# Singlehood

*It's Okay to Be Selfish*

DENNIS S. NICKENS

AKA "THE SPIRITUAL ROMEO"

Copyediting and typesetting: Sally Hanan of Inksnatcher.com

Ordering Information: Quantity sales. Special discounts are available on quantity purchases by corporations, associations, and others. For details, contact the author at the email address above.

Singlehood: It's Okay to Be Selfish/Dennis S. Nickens

Published by Spines
ISBN: 979-8-89569-037-6

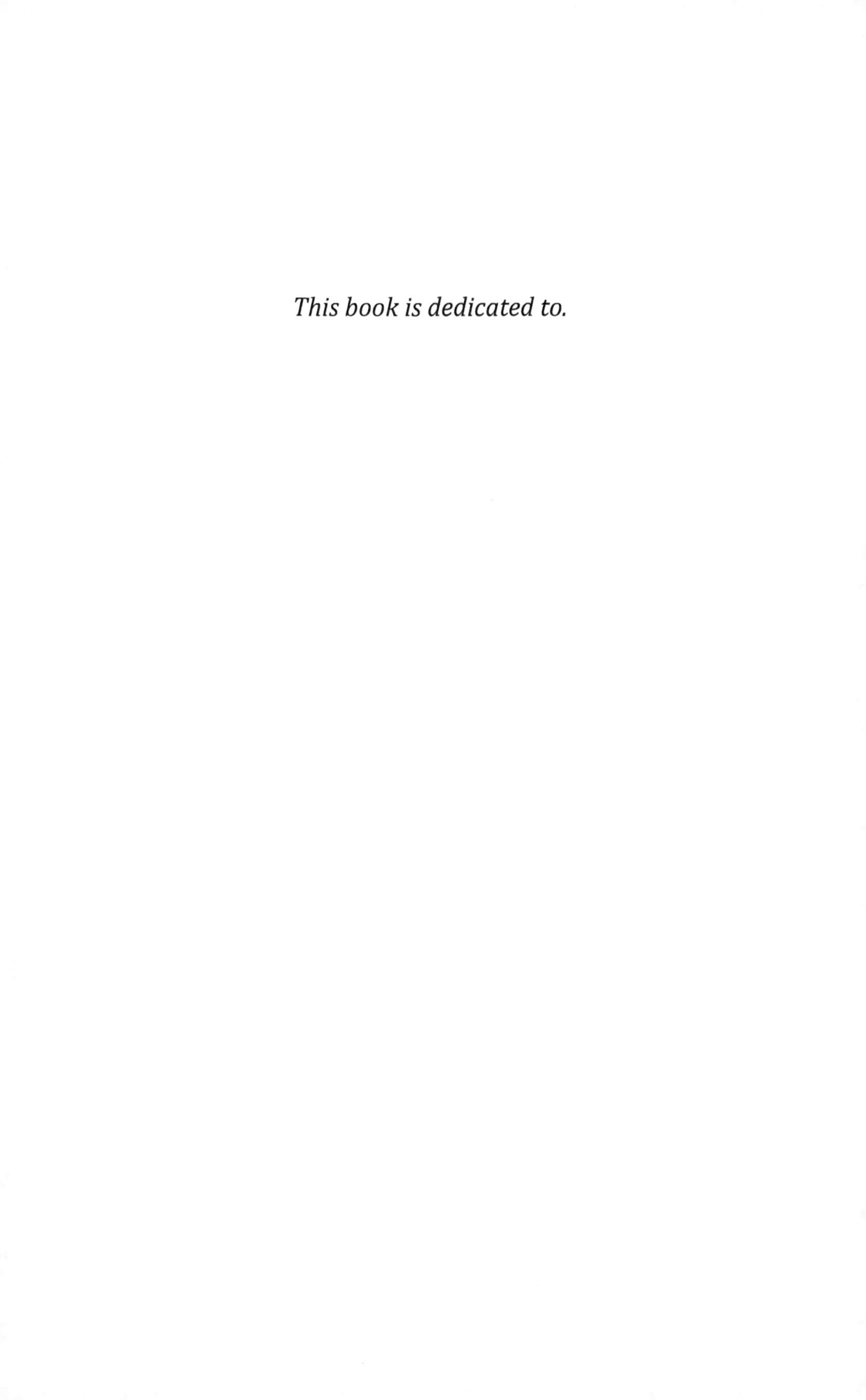

*This book is dedicated to.*

# CONTENTS

# PREFACE

Hello, family. My name is Dennis Nickens, aka *Spiritual Romeo*, an author, public speaker, and relationship encourager. Family, I come before you with a conscious desire to allow God's Word to impact you and take His place at the center of your life. The Word is out, and it will guide you in how to take control over what transpires in your life to bring about a genuine and positive change.

The subtitle of this book is *It's Okay to Be Selfish.* As a single man twice in my life, I have to agree that it's okay only when you focus on yourself for the purpose of becoming anchored in Jesus and set on becoming more like Him. This book is written to help you operate from a healthy place, recognizing the importance of positioning yourself well. When you are in the correct position as a single person, you understand the importance of putting your life and the things you desire at the forefront.

We are all unique individuals, and because we are so uniquely designed, we should only work toward getting into a *healthy* relationship to stay on the path God has designed for us. For this to take place, we have to let God prepare the way and then walk in it; and on the journey we get to prepare ourselves to enter into healthy friendships and relationships.

This is my hope for you. May you take the steps designed just for you and never quit focusing on your path.

Dennis S. Nickens

# — 1 —

# SINGLEHOOD

*The Lord God formed the man of dust from the ground and breathed into his nostrils the breath of life, and the man became a living creature.*
*—Genesis 2:7–8*

I've been single twice in my life—once as a teenager and once as a divorced man—and there's a distinct difference in being single and mature versus being single and immature. I'm sure you can relate.

I was immature when I was in high school, and I dealt with people based on the way I looked at life. I was very disrespectful to girls. I didn't see their true value—how God had designed them. This wasn't how I was raised; my parents raised me to respect women. Nevertheless, because of the individuals I hung around and looked up to, I thought it was acceptable to treat these young ladies with no respect. I saw them as an opportunity, girls

I could take advantage of while they were at a vulnerable place in their lives. I didn't understand the word "value," and neither did they. This part of my life in high school doesn't hold my proudest memories, that's for sure.

People are not in our lives just to use and throw away. And that's why I value my single years as a divorced man so much more. I had matured, and I recognized not only the value I had myself but the value others I interacted with had too. I had a better understanding of what value in everyone meant.

At that point in time, I was living in Atlanta, Georgia, known as the new "chocolate city." There was a multitude of very intelligent and attractive ladies throughout the city, and I got to do life around them. These years were so different because I understood what it meant to value what I stood for. I interacted with people differently and treated them in the way I wanted to be treated—I communicated with them in a way that made them feel important and respected.

I called my sisters queens, and I wanted them to feel like any conversation they had with me would feel safe. I used uplifting words when we talked, even if they did not conduct themselves in a way some judged as being disrespectful to themselves. I saw it as my job to treat them based on their true value and hoped it would help them understand their own value.

My standard as a single mature man was to enjoy life from a place of valuing and respecting myself, so I made a decision that if I was to get involved with someone again, I would maintain those personal standards regardless of how others felt about themselves.

## Perspectives on Value

As you can see, these are two different perspectives of understanding your value—the immature version and the mature perspective. I believe that when you understand your value, your future opens up before you in so many ways. You start functioning as a visible child of God in every area of life, and you become unstoppable.

The main areas of life you operate and grow in are:

- Connections
- Work relationships
- Friendships
- Dating relationships
- Family

And in every single one of these areas, you have the opportunity to grow your:

- Perspective of yourself
- Perspective of others
- Relationship with God
- Character qualities
- Mindset
- Attitude

People call it being single, but it's really not. Every day you are interacting with other people. What they really mean by the word "single" is that you haven't yet found your person—the one you want to do life with 24-7 for the rest of your days. So if you want to maximize your days of singlehood by preparing yourself to be the best spouse ever, you need to learn how to not only get on with other people but how to leave them feeling like they have met someone who has made their day(s) better. Because that's how you want your future spouse to feel every day.

## Ordering Your Inner World

To be able to affect your outer world for good, you need to get your inner world in order. In the diagram below, you can see how I picture this.

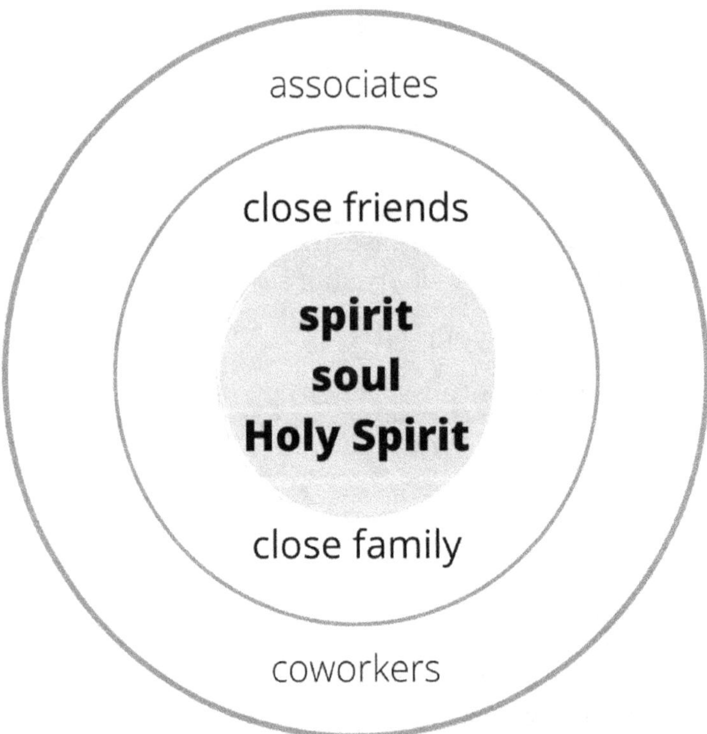


I haven't included dating relationships or courtship in it to keep it to the life of a single person.

## Inner World

THE CORE BEING of every person consists of the spirit and soul, and the Holy Spirit fills every Christian's spirit and soul too.

THE INNER CIRCLE consists of close friends and family. I also call it your inner space, because you only allow those you trust to enter and stay. These are the people you love and value the most, so it makes sense to make this inner space sacred because this is where you invest your best and where you receive the most.

## Outer World

THE OUTER CIRCLE is full of people you know by name. They come in and out of your life and you get to choose who to pull into your inner circle based on what you see in them. You still value and respect them, but you don't invest the same time or attention in them.

THE OUTER WORLD Outside of these circles sit life circumstances—things beyond your ability to control. However, if your inner world is strong, your outer world cannot destroy you. The foundation you stand on will always be ready to rebuild on.

### Your Core Being

When ordering your inner world, you must first take care of your core being. God is the beginning and the end, and getting your core right with God will put everything else in its proper place. You'll have the maturity to know who goes where and who to invest your time in. You'll stand on a firm foundation.

YOUR SPIRIT is the breath of life God breathed into you at conception. You had no choice in this. God decided He wanted you and *boom,* your life began.

*The Lord, who stretched out the heavens and founded the earth and formed the spirit of man within him.*
*- Zechariah 12:1–3*

YOUR SOUL consists of your mind, will, and emotions. You have every choice in deciding what to put in your mind and what to keep out, what to push for and what to run from. Emotions are a little more intricate, but God has a lot of good material to work with.

> Soul: The spiritual, rational and immortal substance in man, which distinguishes him from brutes; that part of man which enables him to think and reason, and which renders him a subject of moral government. The immortality of the soul is a fundamental article of the christian system. Such is the nature of the human soul that it must have a God, an object of supreme affection.
>
> —Webster's Dictionary 1828

THE HOLY SPIRIT is the third Person of the Trinity who lives in you once invited. He gets to infiltrate every part of your spirit and soul, and the more you get to know His voice and recognize His presence, the more aware you are of what to do and how to flow with Him in all your interactions. He is everything God is, so when He lives in you, you have access to all the power, wisdom, love, and faith of heaven. You are one with Him and know Him more every day.

The Spirit searches everything, even the depths of God. For who knows a person's thoughts except the spirit of that person, which is in him? So also no one comprehends the thoughts of God except the Spirit of God. Now we have received not the spirit of the world, but the Spirit who is from God, that we might understand the things freely given us by God. And we impart this in words not taught by human wisdom but taught by the Spirit, interpreting spiritual truths to those who are spiritual. ...

*"For who has understood the mind of the Lord so as to instruct him?" But we have the mind of Christ.*

*—1 Corinthians 2:10–13, 16*

Having the Holy Spirit into your life means your soul gets to be fully alive and whole, but there's a clause in this contract that says you have to surrender your soul to His authority if you want the access to the wholeness He promises. This is easier to do when you know how much thought He put into your uniqueness and how much He wanted you to live here, now, on earth. He has big plans for your life, and everything about your soul is lined up to make it happen once you let God flow with you.

Take the time to reset your core being for your own life, one that only has enough room for you to occupy. No one else can be 100 percent you, so the sooner you figure out who you are, the sooner you can fill that space fully. Singlehood allows you to identify and grow in each area of your life that does not yet reflect the heart and mind of Jesus. When you fill a weak spot with Him, you become even more connected to your God-designed purpose, and even more so when you invite others with the same mindset to grow with you. Working around greatness opens your spiritual eyes, and you start to believe you can accomplish anything in your life.

— 2 —

# YOUR DESIGN ALONE

*The Lord, who stretched out the heavens and founded the earth and formed the spirit of man within him.*
*– Zechariah 12:1–3*

When God created Adam and Eve, He started from a single atom. According to the Bible, Eve was pulled from Adam's side, and she was *formed* into the person God would have her to be (Genesis 2:21–23). God *created* Adam from the dirt and Eve from his side, but He never went through that process again with anyone. He never created anyone the way He created Adam and Eve. God took the dust of the ground and added his breath of life and Adam appeared whole and ready to go. He then shaped Eve from Adam's rib. Once birthed, Adam and Eve would go through a lot more to be shaped into the people they became. In the same way, God planned out your one-on-one developmental process and identity that you now get to mature into being. When you are connected with your initial purpose and walk with God, you are formed into the person God intended you to be.

My purpose here is to encourage you to allow your original design and your developmental process to work together. Gain a clear understanding of how you were formed, but also—more importantly—*why* you were created. Then find the areas that need improving, the things you need to get better at, and ask God to develop those in you. When you let this happen, you open yourself up to God's blessing, and you learn how to not only embrace your single status but also get excited about it.

When you know God is your foundation, you understand better the process you have to go through to get to be who really you are. God not only created you in His likeness; he put a lot inside you that He knew would grow and develop—to the point where you start to look and act like Him. Do not allow anyone to dictate who or what you should emulate. You are a person formed in the image of the Creator of heaven and earth. Imitate and follow Him alone. You are an ink pen in God's hand, and with you He draws pictures, writes down information, and impacts the lives of others. God is the greatest One. He encourages you and tells you every day that you are destined for greatness. Just think about it—out of all of the millions of sperm cells, you were the one who was created to be you.

## You Are Diverse

The Father created you to be very diverse, unique, and different from any other person He created. When you live in Him and He lives in you, you're a different kind of specimen. You're not of this world. You are just dwelling in this space for a season.

You do not have to strive to be like any other person or try your best to emulate their persona; He sent you down here to be a standalone, unique being, different in all aspects. Naturally, being different might seem like a hell of a task, but with the agency of God's spirit, it is a very attainable possibility. He sent you down here to make a change that will touch the four corners of the world, so undergo a transformation that is pleasing to God. Become fully His. Move where the Spirit tells you to move. Just like the wind, be flexible and welcoming to the biddings and the urgings of the Lord. Anyone who is of God must be like the wind, ready to go where the Spirit leads. "He will come like a rushing stream, which the wind of the Lord drives" (Isaiah 59:19).

God does not want you to be rigid in your ways. He wants you to be rigid only in not moving out of His will. Live according to the leading of the Spirit. Are you afraid things may turn sour? The Bible said, "Let God be true though every one were a liar, as it is written, 'That you may be justified in your words, and prevail when you are judged'" (Romans 3:4). So you're going to be victorious. You're going to be successful. That's what the Word of God says. That's what it said is going to happen to you.

Anyone who tries to stop you from doing what the Father has called you to do is a liar. Your Father has not called you to stop. To be swayed by others' opinions in your life is not the will of the Father for your life. He said He would bring people in your life to build you up and to ensure you are successful (Ephesians 4). That's what your Father said because He called you into the partnership of sonship and into the family of God. And that's not just about the people in your church, it's Christians everywhere.

## You Are Special

Look into someone's eyes and let them know they are special. Have them read God's Word, especially those places where the Lord made great promises to them. Teach them to read it and apply it to their lives, knowing they're special when they go about their daily businesses. Create that change in them and have them believe it with all their hearts.

Your Father laid things out for you to be victorious. There's nothing someone can give to you to make you excel more than what the Lord has given you. You are more than a conqueror. That's why the Father created you. Don't let anyone talk down to you because you are trying to excel in everything that you do. Even when you apply for a job, expect someone to see you as a masterful creation designed to fill that role. That's the way you should think about yourself. Don't let anybody tell you anything different. Be sober minded and clear in the way you think. Be energized by the Spirit and motivated about doing what the Father wants you to do. Be watchful over the things you do with your life. Be on your guard and on your spiritual best behavior. Conduct yourself in a way that's pleasing unto the Father. He's called you into this. He's called you to be different from all others. "You are a chosen race, a royal priesthood, a holy nation, a people for his own possession, that you may proclaim the excellencies of him who called you out of darkness into his marvelous light" (1 Peter 2:9).

## You Are Unique

Man, you are unique in your set of qualities. You exist in only one particular package. No one can live this life out for you. You are a sole example for others to see. You are singular and not plural. That means the Father didn't call you to multiply you. He needs a single, individual, one-on-one relationship with you to develop you as He has designed you to live. That is the sort of relationship you have with your Father in heaven.

The Father is big enough to have a one-on-one relationship with you and every one of His children. That's unique. That's wonderful. David said, "I praise you for I am fearfully and wonderfully made." We are all wonderfully and fearfully made, made with a conscious effort that depicts the intentionality of the Father who has called us unto glory. He loves us that much. He loves us with a love that cannot be quantified or measured using any scale known to man.

All God ever wants from you is to acknowledge you are wonderfully and fearfully made, and you will start reaping the results you want for your life. Yes, you are made in His likeness and image. Say it for yourself. You have control over what comes out of your mouth, so speak it for yourself because you have a spiritual connection and relationship with God.

We can all eat this Word for ourselves. We need to read it.

> I count everything as loss because of the surpassing worth of knowing Christ Jesus my Lord. … [having] the righteousness from God that depends on faith … Not that I have already obtained this or am already perfect, but I press on to make it my own, because Christ Jesus has made me his own. Brothers, I do not consider that I have made it my own. But one thing I do: forgetting what lies behind and straining forward to what lies

> ahead, I press on toward the goal for the prize of the upward call of God in Christ Jesus.
>
> —Philippians 3:8–9, 12–14

You've already been perfected, courtesy of the substitutionary work of Christ on the cross of Calvary. Keep pressing to the mark because Jesus Christ said He has made you His own. Let this realization get you energized to do things more in the way the Lord wants them done.

God has made you His own? Look forward, brother. Do not be worried about your past. It has passed. Press toward the goal for the prize from your Lord and Savior, Jesus Christ. Pray you are part of His body. Pray you're connected with His Son. I hope to see what He has for you. If you earnestly seek God's face, He will reveal it to you. Read this Word of God, family; read it and apply it for yourself. And when you go about your daily journey, live as the special, uniquely made person you are. God bless you.

It's so important for you to be energized by His Word and His Spirit so that His breath burns within you and helps you live out your life purpose. When He energizes you, you cannot die. As long as you're screaming, howling, and yelling some form of energy through your body, you cannot die. You can't leave this earth. So just think about it. Anything you desire in your heart has the energy in your spirit to bring it to life. Continue to give it life so your destiny can come to pass. The Father put it in you and it did not come from any man.

Be energized about what the Father has given you. He didn't give it to you by mistake. He gave it to you on purpose, and you are the only person who can handle what the Father has given to you.

The truth is that God has always indicated He will reveal why you were created to be on this earth and what your purpose is. Develop a relationship with Him and spend more time in fellowship with Him. Seek understanding from Him. The Holy Spirit will confirm that voice in you, and it will be like no other voice you've ever heard. He will say to you, "You know, son/daughter, I created you." When you listen to that voice, your mind's transformation will get you to look at things so differently.

## Your Purpose and Destiny

There's something special about you that makes you stand out in the crowd, something unique about you that the world needs. Understand your value and realize that you are more than what the average person thinks. God is present in your life, and He desires to develop everything He has put in you to the point in your life when people say you look and act like Him.

You are essential to this world. The Father took the time to breathe His life into you. You are created exactly the way you are because what you have inside you is essential right now and at every moment throughout your life. You are the reflection of a purpose God planted inside you, therefore God both requires and encourages you to connect to *His* expectations instead of your own. He believes that something good will come from His investment, so step into what He expects of you to live your best life. When you have an understanding of *what* God has created, you will understand *why* you were created.

When you're single, you have time to focus on the things that are beneficial to your development and growth, like seeking your purpose. Looking for your purpose is like medicine to your soul. It might not digest well or taste good some days, but when you choose to endure, life gets richer. Find out about it, and in due time and season, you will see your life shifting toward it in a beneficial direction because you know the direction you're heading in.

## Your Mission

As a single person, you need to understand your mission—the bigger picture that God calls you to be subject to. The Father wants you to be led by the Word of God as you fulfil your mission. Understand your assignment. As you focus on it, God will teach you the way you should go. First learn how to be an effective follower. A good leader will provide you with information that's designed to build your knowledge up.

As you learn, focus your attention on understanding why that leader is doing what he or she is doing. Do not be afraid to ask them questions pertaining to concerns you may have. However, do not make the mistake of observing someone and jumping to assumptions about why they do what they do.

There is a difference in having an idea and following a mission. An idea is a thought that comes and goes with no firm foundation to it. It's a tempting idea that can get you off track. A mission is a God-given, foundational concept. It establishes itself deep down in your core and gives you spiritual nutrients. But more importantly, the mission comes from a source that's bigger than what you can see. This source knows you better that you know yourself. He is the Creator of all things, and He is the one who understands what is needed to help you evolve. God the Father created the seed of your mission. The beautiful thing about this seed is that it's unique in nature and it was created as a reflection of the first Adam's seed. God created your mission from a place that can never be duplicated. Your mission is exclusive in nature based on you being someone who cannot be duplicated. The more you understand your unique qualities, the more you will build what's needed to complete your assignments.

When it comes to being part of the kingdom family, understand that you are separated and you are different. You came here to serve in whatever role the Father created for you. You can be excited! I'm telling you, family, you can get excited about the things the Father's calling you to do. Your spiritual eyes will open to see that what He is giving you is not in vain. It's set up for a purpose. You are set up to complete your mission. Let's go!

# – 3 –

# YOUR MISSION ALONE

*For Adam there was not found a helper comparable to him.*
*– Matthew 28:19*

Your life needs to be structured around being a servant to the Word of God. Those who understand the Word of God will understand that God created you to be the example of His character to the world. When you place yourself in His structure correctly, you will be like the church—you'll provide answers to those who are lost.

Jesus had no issues in following through by giving His life for a cause that was bigger than who He was. He did not hesitate; He did what he had to. His focus was on His mission. Ultimately, Christ is the true example of leadership, and He showed us what we need to do to function in our divine authority. Christ loved us so much that He gave His life for us. He did something nobody else would or could do. His main focus was to serve us and help us thrive. Our mission is the same.

Don't waver in your thinking or your actions when it comes to rendering service to people. Don't waver in the love you have for affecting lives. Do what you do in love through the anointing that flows over you and through you. God has anointed you to stand in your rightful position of doing right by your Father. Your positioning is key. As a child of God, you do not stand in the front or the back, you stand right beside the Father who will never leave you or forsake you. Your mission statement will assist you as you operate in a role that may seem strange to others.

As a servant unto the Lord, God is the one who wears the crown and whom you bow down to. There are going to be times where you will find yourself in a position that makes you feel uncomfortable. When this happens, I encourage you to put your trust in God and His ability to pull something out of you that will help you. It's Gods mission is to help you understand what this word "servanthood" truthfully is—the ability to serve through actions that speak louder than words. You can say one thing, but if you are not a reflection of it, your actions won't mirror the true meaning of the words that come out of your mouth.

You are the point man or woman, the forerunner for Christ. Your vision is clear, and you understand the goal of leading by example. You lead from the front and not behind. When you have no insecurity, you have no issues in taking the lesser role of servant. You know this will allow you to see situations from a different angle that gives you a better understanding about them.

An effective Christian needs to be balanced. You should desire to build upon what has been placed in you. Take a hold of the mission and run with it rather than follow your fleshly desires. If you get caught up in yourself, your vision can be askew because what you perceive as accurate is not what God sees as truth. Your vision can be distorted if you focus on the incorrect thing. Your growth is based upon your spiritual thoughts and your spiritual walk. Your thoughts can lead you to an awkward position if you focus on the wrong thing. When you have God, you submit yourself to the mission He's given you versus the sporadic ideas that run through your mind.

When you run with His mission, God helps you understand Him better. Isaiah 55 states that God's thoughts are not your thoughts. God makes it clear He does not think like mankind. The Word of God shows us God's thoughts, and the more we read it, the more we align our own thought with His and gain a mature mind. When you subject yourself to serve the mission of God, you serve His thoughts and plans. Having a relationship with God includes having the Holy Spirit take up residence in your life to help you understand the thoughts of God. He inspires you to seek understanding and grab a hold of the significance of the Word of God.

At times you could find yourself looking at something one way and the spirit of God looks at it in another way. As a servant, go into a situation knowing *who* you are and *why* you are there, but be willing to follow the flow of the Spirit when it comes to deciding *what* to do. For example, let's say you desire to take a pathway you feel is right but the spirit of God says nope. You have a choice to make. Either you are going to go the way you feel is right or go in the direction you know is right. This is the battleground most people struggle with, but true Christians lean toward His will more than toward their desires.

Being obedient to the mission will guide you through the process. It will help you see things your natural eyes are limited in seeing. God knows everything, and He gives you a mission that's linked to His spirit. As a true son or daughter of God, you are subject to Him. His ways are higher than your thoughts. There are so many different ways people go about conducting their business, but the only right way is God's way—the way that's higher than the way your thoughts come up with. Undisciplined people believe a way without a plan is built upon ideas, but submitting to your God-given mission is the only way to go.

Be cautious about where your thoughts lead you. Hopefully I have helped you understand that not all worldly thoughts are worth adopting. Only take on thoughts that come from a tested source. God has given you a mission you can commit to, and working towards it will balance your pursuit of your calling.

The calling upon your life cannot be mixed with injections of the thoughts of the world. That's like putting poison in a pure glass of water. Your mission is to have your thoughts flow in the pure water of God's thoughts. God is trying to prevent you from taking poison into your life, which includes telling you to stay away from someone venomous and absolutely telling you to never enter into a relationship with certain people. That's why you need to vet the people trying to enter your life. Ensure they're not trying to put venom into your life. We want to keep those things out. You want to be guarded by the Word of God because nothing stands higher than that. The calling upon your life is higher than your thoughts. You need to be careful to not take on the thoughts of the world because they make you function in error, hinder your development, and hurt the people closest to you.

Understand the importance of ensuring God's mission is directing your life—so the people connected with you can be blessed. The anointing you have been given is not just for you but also for the people who are connected to you. You are anointed to do something amazing by being an effective follower of Jesus. There is a reason and purpose for the people who come into your life. Make sure you use your spiritual eyes to analyze people and be honest about what you see.

## Mission Directives

In order to move on, you need the following:

### 1. Balance

Following your mission requires balance. Know when it's your time to lead or submit. You cannot always be at the forefront because to function properly with your mission, you understand where you are strong and where you are weak. When you understand this, there is no need for you to be in a lead position all the time—that's when you let others who are strong in those areas help you develop. This is how you stay on track with your mission.

Be blessed as you allow your mission to move forward and you do what you were called to do—to lead, serve, function, and operate freely in your calling. When you do this, you do not get caught up in yourself, and you understand your life is not about who you are but about the mission at hand and how you are uniquely called to fulfill it.

When you try to make yourself more important than the mission, you are in the wrong position. You have to allow the spirit of God to build you up and allow you to function in your strengths. When Jesus was at a wedding with his mother, Mary wanted Him to take care of the wine shortage. In John 2:4 he called Mary "woman" and not Mother. He said, "Woman, what does this have to do with me? My time has not come." But remember what Mary did next. "His mother said to the servants, 'Do whatever he tells you'" (v. 5). Here, Mary showed herself functioning and maneuvering in her role, and telling people where they should go. She was in a leadership role, but she understood Jesus had to do something for the wedding to go to the next level, so she went to Him knowing she would have to do whatever He said, and Jesus turned the water into wine.

In all looking at your current relationships, you need Jesus to turn your water into wine. That's what Jesus does best. Once you taste Jesus, there's nothing that tastes sweeter than Him. He is true and was telling the truth when He claimed He would take your life and transform it to please the Father. You need to submit to His authority if you want the water of your own relationships turned to wine.

## 2. Set the Example

If you're a leader, you have to understand that true leadership is very important. You don't have to tell people you're in charge. When you do that, you are immature in your thinking. You don't know how to function as a true leader. Your actions speak louder than words, and you have to be an example of the Father to people on this earth. He told us not to allow anyone to despise our youth, but to set an example in speech, conduct, love, faith, and purity (1 Timothy 4:12). Those points are what leadership is all about.

Make sure you function properly in your speech and conversation. Make sure you conduct yourself properly and embrace love from the position of being mature enough to handle the pressures of life. There are times when you'll say things that may not feel right, but if you're setting the example, stand and don't move until you are sure what you are about to do is right because people may be watching and following your example.

The Word of God actively requires your willingness to be a servant of the authority of God. Be mature enough to handle the purpose and calling on your life in a humble way.

Take a stand on obedience. Move towards God's will for your life. As an effective leader, be accountable for your actions and eliminate excuses. Live and dwell in greatness. Declare that you understand you may not be perfect, but you will not complain about where you are. If you make a mistake, own up to it and learn how to get past it. It is the Word of God that lifts you up and changes you for the better.

### 3. Your Mission Is Not Your Competition.

I often observe people competing with one another. You have to operate in oneness with your mission, not with someone else's mission. The chief adversary is the Devil, and that's who you should be trying to get at.

This is not a competition about who scores. All things work out for good and in your favor when you obey God. As people link up with you, they become members of your team. As an effective teammate, it should not matter who scores as long as you are all supporting the same mission. The power of God in your lives brings you together as one unit, and there's nothing the enemy can do to stop you from scoring.

The Word builds you up and enables you to run over every thought that stands in your way because the Word is true, and everything else is a lie.

Don't handle your business as if you are trying to compete with the person you're dating (Philippians 2:3) That's not your role. Get your thoughts under control. It is more significant and beneficial to be subject to your connections—the ones you have chosen to pour into your life. When you get caught up in your feelings, you become immature and start functioning like a little child. Get back to your mission, the one you took a holy vow to stand on, and be unwilling to waver in your thoughts.

You aren't supposed to opt out of a God-given mission, nor do anything that will jeopardize it, when you have the One who is the source of all strength. The enemy's job is to get you off track and look at things in a way that is not true. Don't deviate from your purpose nor feed your mind with tumultuous thoughts. Be mature and seek comfort by allowing the light of God's Word to lead you to your destiny.

### 4. Being on The Same Page

As a powerful leader, your mission is to fall in love with the understanding that you and your mission are one. God created your mission for the purpose of protecting you. In knowing you are protected, you have to be willing to find balance in being okay with not being in charge at times and serving instead. Following the mission God has for your life relaxes your mind. You are led by the Source who leads the way. Be willing to embrace your leading-serving balance and learn how to run this race called life together with those you have chosen to align yourself with.

"Have this mind among yourselves, which is yours in Christ Jesus" (Philippians 2: 5). Jesus understands family. You have the mind of Christ. You can think and function alike. Since Christ thought like God, why do you find walking round and talking like a winner problematic? "The glory that you have given me I have given to them, that they may be one even as we are one, I in them and you in me, that they may become perfectly one, so that the world may know that you sent me and loved them even as you loved me" (John 17: 22–23).

Maturity makes us recognize our equality with each other, standing side by side. God didn't make a mistake in giving you two ears but only one mouth. There's a time to speak and a time to listen. When you incorporate balance in your life, you learn how to speak at the right time and how to operate at a powerful level. Act like a godly leader. Seek out His holy face. Find the treasure of seeking Jesus Christ and let Him be the Lord of your life. Most important—let Him reign over your relationships. Don't cause your flesh to destroy the relationships He is trying to build.

### 5. Seek Greatness

Seek out the face of God every day to excel. Don't accept mediocracy in your life. Ensure those in your inner circle are able to touch God's greatness in you by reaching your full potential. First thing in the morning, encourage yourself by speaking life into the atmosphere, making an announcement to the spiritual realm of what is about to take place. Elevate your vocabulary and speak words that are going to elevate your thinking. You can speak and talk like Jesus spoke and talk (John 8 and 14).

The mission within you belongs to the Father. As you develop a better relationship with the mission God has for your life, you become comfortable in going through the process of being formed. Standing in the position of authority and on the mission leading you, you can reply like Jesus to any circumstance: "Has God not been for me all this time? And did you not recall that the mission I'm running behind is the Father's? Can't you see that what I'm standing on is the Father? Can't you see the mission is more important than myself?" See the mission in you rather than yourself. That is what will spur you on.

Ask God for spiritual eyes to see the mission. Jesus said anyone who has seen Him has seen the Father, so when you see the mission over your life through the Word, you have seen the Father. When you understand these things, you're going to be great. That's when you go to the next level.

The Holy Spirit leads us into a better understanding of who He who we uniquely are. We are made to be different from the rest of the world. When we have fully understood we can be different, the next thing for us is to strive to fulfil our mission. The fact that God, in His infinite wisdom, commanded it in the Scriptures means it is very much attainable. Your life can be perfect when you become different according to the recommendations of the Word of the Lord.

# — 4 —

# BE SELFISH ABOUT YOUR RELATIONSHIP WITH GOD

*God created man in his own image, in the image of God he created him; male and female he created them.*
*– Genesis 1:26–27*

The type of relationship I have my heavenly Father requires me to be held accountable for my actions. I'm committed to Him and He's committed to me. Based on this, we have dialogues that open my mind to be able to see things no one else is capable of seeing. I have learned to trust the process.

I trust the information He gives me. My goal is to make myself available to receive endless amount of information. Once I digest what has been poured into me, I make sure the information that comes out of me is pleasing to His ears—because I know how valuable the relationship is and I am unwilling to do things that would damage what has been built.

Do not get it twisted. I have missed the mark and gotten things wrong more times than I have gotten them right. I trust and believe that I have a Father who loves me. He is making sure that I am prepared to move forward and helping me move. It's wisdom to be guided by Him, building a relationship that cannot be broken. It is like tying knots together on a string. The more knots you tie, the harder it becomes to break.

A relationship with your everlasting Father should be a relationship that has you feeling like you matter, just like any relationships you have with others should. You can't build relationships with anyone else properly if your relationship with God is not solid first. As a single person, be unwilling to allow *anyone* to destroy the relationship you have with Him. Ultimately, He is the only One who has your best interests at heart.

Being single should free your mind from the pressures of life, not add to them. You shouldn't feel that you lack some secret formula on how to be attractive to the opposite sex. The most attractive thing about a solid relationship is when both partners have a solid foundation in Him. In God's eyes, you are the core piece of solid foundation when He's your center. Accept that you can only be a healthy partner when He is your primary source. Be ready to pay the cost for choosing this path because it can be tempting to let go when bad things happen. Certain friends will move out of your life, you might be let go from a job you thought was permanent, and, at times, you might suffer through tragic events you cannot understand. Regardless of what transpires in your life, you must maintain a consistent thinking pattern of trust in

God. When you love Him and trust Him, you know without a doubt that everything will work for your good, and that you'll get to live out the amazing life He has planned for you. "We know that in all things God works for the good of those who love him, who have been called according to his purpose" (Romans 8:28).

Do not have any fear of the Enemy. Let your fear only be of the Lord because you understand your relationship with Him is worth more than any other relationship you have with the world. This is how it should be. This is the way. Live in truth and take control of your life. Turn in the correct direction like God's Word in the book of Proverbs admonishes, when it said, "Turn away from the evil one." Who is the evil one? He is the one trying to get you to do the things that are outside of what destined for you. Your Enemy is the one trying to get you to disbelieve you were created for a mission and that that mission creates a pathway that leads to your purpose-filled life.

Regardless of what happens, do not worry because you have a solid relationship with your Lord and Savior. Go ahead and grow your relationship with Him so you can comfortably adjust to whatever situation may come. Encourage yourself in the knowledge that you will always be completely unwilling to be moved away from living out your destiny.

As Christians, we have to understand that whatever we do is not about us but about Him, who called us to glory. Our lives are about the divine order of things He has predestined for us. We frequently mess things up because we often rely on our judgment and perception when setting our things in order, but when we trust Him enough to order our footsteps, He sets our feet in the right direction, just like the Word of God says. "The

Spirit entered into me and set me on my feet, and I heard him speaking to me" (Ezekiel 2:2).

God wants our lives to follow His divine order because He knows and sees us better than we see ourselves; He calls us peculiar or unique people. The most important person you can identify with is Jesus. He is the person who has the receipt for the transaction He made on the cross of Calvary. He is the person who has the final say in our lives. That's the Person we should run after. He is important in our lives and without Him, we are all goners.

## Sonship

Don't try to be like anybody else. Be who the Father has called you to be. He has called you into sonship. When you get revelatory knowledge and understanding about who you are and what the Word of God says about you, you realize the Father did not call you to be a Christian, He called you unto sonship.

> As indeed he says in Hosea,
> "Those who were not my people I will call 'my people,'
> and her who was not beloved I will call 'beloved.'"
> "And in the very place where it was said to them, 'You are not my people,'
> there they will be called 'sons of the living God.'"
>
> —Romans 9:25–26

His relationship with you is His greatest joy. When you receive Jesus Christ, His blood comes upon your life and you become part of Christ's bloodline. The Father is always looking out for His children, for you!, so jump for joy because this is a very privileged position He has called you into. You have Him in your life and He's upon your life, so get excited about every step you take and every place you go.

You are a game changer because you have the Son in you. When the Father sees you, He doesn't see Michael or Jane. He sees His child full of His nature; He doesn't look at our old nature. He casts His gaze at the Christ in us. When we understand these things, we can read God's Word differently and get to know what He wants us to do in our lives. Even if you're not someone who believes in His Word, God's Word will still make you a game changer if and when you apply it correctly in your life. When you read God's Word as it applies to you, you'll think differently.

God loves you more than you can love yourself. It doesn't matter what you've gone through because God's love is in your life, teaching you how to love yourself. You need to love yourself before you can love anybody else. The love thing from the Father is upon you.

What does this sort of love look like? It looks like the Father's embrace and the Father's loving presence you'll feel after receiving it. This is an experiential love, so when you feel it, you'll have a better understanding of what love is. He promised to touch your heart, mind, and spirit to feel what love truly is. It is a rewarding experience.

## Made in His Image

God didn't call you to be as the other brother or sister over there, and He doesn't want you to do or say the same thing someone else said or did. Dare to be perfect even as your heavenly Father is perfect (Matthew 5:48). The Father has called you perfect, a saint even (1 Corinthians 1:2). If anyone came to you and said, "No, you can't be perfect," say, "That's not what my Father says about me. He says I can be perfect because He's perfecting me to be what He wants." When He created you, He created you to be a perfect reflection of Him. By being a reflection of Him, you should do what He has intended you do.

> You, who once were alienated and enemies in your mind by wicked works, yet now He has reconciled in the body of His flesh through death, to present you holy, and blameless, and above reproach in His sight—if indeed you continue in the faith, grounded and steadfast, and are not moved away from the hope of the gospel which you heard.
>
> —Colossians 1:21–23

That's the thing. When you go about doing things, you will be energized because you do not think of doing them in your name but in the name of your Father who sent you. When you diligently seek His face, you are going to be steadfast and effective. As James said, "Let steadfastness have its full effect, that you may be perfect and complete, lacking in nothing" (James 1:4). The Father said, "I called you to be perfect and complete." The Father said you were perfect, and your complete. Everything you need for you to excel, the Father said, "I had given it to you." It's in your hand. You do not lack anything. That's what He said.

You are created differently. Your life has been laid out before you. You are on a mission fighting to get through to the vision in front of you. By the word of His mouth, you are different because He made you so!

Reading God's Word isn't just about reading; it holds the practical knowledge you need to apply in your life to make your uniqueness work for you. Following His Word makes results possible because you are divinely connected to Him and His spirit. The benefits we'll enjoy from being intimately connected to the Lord of Glory are enormous!

I pray that you have a desire to be like Jesus. He walked upon the earth making every moment count. Just like Jesus, be the person who understands that the things you can accomplish are significant. With Him in you, you will understand the importance of valuing your time and valuing your own position in it.

## Live under His Authority

Living on this earth and operating under His umbrella of greatness requires you to put on the full armor of God and allow His authority to rest upon your shoulders. The beautiful thing about the type of relationship you have with your heavenly Father is that since He created you, He understands how much weight you can carry on them. He also understands what's required of Him to get you to the place you need to be.

## Letting Go

If our relationship with God is to be whole, we must forgive others because He's forgiven us. We can't bring any of that poison into our relationship with Him. It's a big deal to God.

*"Forgive us our debts, as we also have forgiven our debtors."*
*—Matthew 6:12*
*"If you forgive others their trespasses, your heavenly Father will also forgive you, but if you do not forgive others their trespasses, neither will your Father forgive*

*your trespasses."*
*—Matthew 6:14–15*

Right now, take a mental journey into the deepest part of your mind. Think of some of the worst things that have been done to you by a certain individual. Still on that island of thoughts, remember the prison in which these thoughts caged you. Think of how they have been hurting you. Consider the untold joy this state has deprived you of and the emotional chaos it has plunged you into. Think of the time and resources this state of mind has robbed you of over the days, months, and years. Think of that person right now in your mind. The burning question is, can you forgive this person?

The truth is that forgiving the people who have hurt you and letting go of the terrible situations they put you through has not always been easy. It is even more difficult if the person is not remorseful of their deeds or they do not know the degree of damage they have caused. But carefully consider this: If you keep harboring your ill feelings about their actions against you, it wouldn't still change the fact that they would still be out there living their lives and being insensitive to your feelings. While you keep entertaining these grudges and permitting the ill feelings to take their toll on your progress, they're probably out partying. You are there keeping grudges and they are out there dancing.

The truth of the matter is that the situations can only go from bad to worse with Ill Feelings Entertainment. The liberating truth is that you can learn how to let go of anything bad that was done to you. Do this as soon as possible. It will free you from the shackles of unforgiveness and you can set your life on the one-way road of progress and open more doors to your happiness and fulfillment.

Below are some of the obvious benefits of letting go and the benefits they come with.

## Freedom

Letting go of things that hurt you fills you with a feeling of freedom. Hurt is a burden to our soul, and if not properly checked, it can lead to a deep and undesirable mess. When you learn to let go of hurtful things, you adopt a new state of mind that comes with the ability to forget the things that have been done to you by the aggressor. Going by this logic, the benefit is far greater for you than the person you forgive when you chose to let go unconditionally.

## Optimism

A lot has been written about the charming disposition of an optimistic mind. To achieve success in all walks of life, this way of being should be adopted. People who are quick to let go of the past are generally optimists. They are happy and grateful for the people in their lives, even though these same people occasionally hurt them. They tend to not take most things personally, even when it seems like a personal attack. They are quick to address the things that need to be addressed and then come back to their defining purpose. If you want to be like them, you should get busy doing the same thing.

## Strength

It is no surprise to see that many people who forgive often are some of the strongest people emotionally. When you make a practice of constantly forgiving people, it becomes easier to do so in the future, and if you practice letting go of bigger faults, then bigger faults become easier to let go of in the future too. The truth has always been that it's never easy to forgive, but when you face a difficult situation that requires you to let go of an offence for the sake of your peace, you can assure yourself that you have faced even worse situations and you have scaled them because you forgave. When you do this, just like magic, everything will suddenly become easier for you.

You may be thinking: *Well, forgiving someone and letting go of difficult situations isn't a bad idea, but how exactly do I do it? You can't say you let go and then everything just settles itself. No! It can't be that easy.* You are probably correct. It is surely not a deal that'll be killed with one shot. One of the best things to remember when you are trying to let go is that forgiveness is a process.

Sometimes in your relationships, you'll feel your friend or dating partner offended you; in that case, you'll need to learn how to forgive them and let go … every time.

## Relationships Built God's Way

An ordinary relationship is built based on how the world perceives it, and the world has plenty of opinions and advice on what should go into a relationship, even though most people are pessimistic about a great relationship even being possible. But when you apply God's Word to your relationship with people, you can expect an extraordinary relationship since your relationship is founded on the word and will of God. And as you know, the Word and His will are beyond the ordinary. They are extraordinary, and with your relationship hinged on Him, you'll enjoy the benefit of extraordinary relationships with people.

People call something ordinary because it is not special to them. Ordinary things are ordinary because there is nothing extraordinary about them. But the Bible says you were created for a purpose, and when you live from that purpose, God's dynamite power automatically comes upon your relationships with people and they become extraordinary. That's what it's about. Give your relationships the opportunity to be explosive. Every time you come together with people you share something in common with, you don't just get excited about being close to the person; you get to share the illumination that flows from your life. That's what you want.

# — 5 —

# BE SELFISH ABOUT KINGDOM-MINDED OBEDIENCE

*Therefore a man shall leave his father and his mother and hold fast to his wife, and they shall become one flesh.*
*– Genesis 2:24*

The information contained in this manual will take your relationship life, and by extension some other parts of your life, to the next level. Your spiritual eyesight will help you see every step He desires you to take toward getting to your predestined destination. I strongly believe that receiving His wise way of seeing things is the next step in the process of living out your life successfully.

All you have been going through is part of your growth in a divinely orchestrated process. When you accept your past as the process to the ultimate destination He is leading you to, you will not take it all for granted. The Almighty Father can find the gold in anything happening in your life.

## The Kingdom Operates Differently

Being kingdom minded means you realize and accept the divine plan for your life, and you set your heart to it irrespective of what you have gone through in life. Engage yourself in the kingdom and its actualization through you. One man who has mentored me well through his book is Dr Myles Munroe, who has authored many books about the kingdom of God. Find authors you respect and learn as much as you can about how the kingdom of God can operate through you.

One of the primary topics Jesus taught on was God's kingdom and His will and how we could make it manifest on earth. He started many parables with the words "The Kingdom of heaven is like..." You can find them in:

- Mark 4: 26–29
- Matthew 13: 44–46
- Matthew 13: 31–43
- Matthew 13: 47–52
- Matthew 25: 1–13
- Matthew 22: 1–14
- Matthew 13: 24–30
- Matthew 20: 1–16
- Matthew 18: 21–35

Jesus implored his disciples to do His Father's will on earth as it is done in heaven. He wanted us to understand the kingdom construct He wants us to live in. He said the kingdom would come when His will on earth had been done. Everything in your committed relationship has been settled in heaven, in line with the will of your heavenly Father.

To expand your understanding of what the kingdom is and to take possession of what He has kept in store for you, you must know His mandate for your life. Just like the Holy Bible puts it, "Seek first the kingdom of God and his righteousness" (Matthew 6:33). Nothing else can be any clearer! Seek out His will for your life first. Make it your priority above everything else!

The enduring will of the Father has always been that every one of His children seek His will. Seek His kingdom and His righteousness, and every good thing you can imagine be added unto you. What am I talking about? What is going to be added to you? The very plans He has for your life realized. To have this involves being where you are supposed to be at the right time with the right people.

In order for you to construct a "kingdom," you need the mind of a king. When you are kingdom minded, you run your life and do things completely differently from the way people who are not of the kingdom do them. Be a kingdom-minded person. Even when you are sick, continue to speak kingdom things out of your mouth, even when it comes to your finances. Life is all about the kingdom, putting things together in line with the Scriptures, and obeying His direct ordinances.

## Reflect the Kingdom

God placed His action plan in your heart to guide you in the way you are supposed to go. You have the blueprint to construct yourself under a spiritual umbrella that's designed to protect you from destructive measures. Your mission is to obey the King who lights desires in hearts. Become a strategic thinker by not getting caught up in the desire of the flesh but of the Spirit who understands the flesh. It's all about His glory, and having the kingdom mindset and doing the will of your Father will bring Him great glory. Make Him all you set your heart to, even when He calls you to assists others. We are to follow His spiritual instructional manual. In order to be the best, be a reflection of the kingdom. Make it part of your life and live life with all of your being encapsulated in Him.

The kingdom of heaven does not have anything to do with other unrelated aspects of your life such as your age, but it has everything to do with your life. It has everything to do with the manifestation of the will of the Almighty on earth as it is done in heaven.

## A Spiritual Kingdom

Make sure everything you do is about the kingdom. Jesus said His kingdom is heavenly and has nothing to do with the earth realm. What's your level of understanding on this statement, and of God's intention for your life?

His kingdom is an eternal kingdom. It is a spiritual kingdom. That's why slicing the high priest's servant's ear off when they came to arrest Jesus was pointless (John 18:10). That's not how we bring the kingdom of heaven to earth. The King of Glory told His disciples "My kingdom is not of this world. If my kingdom were of this world, my servants would have been fighting, that I might not be delivered over to the Jews. But my kingdom is not from the world" John 18:36). And that is true. There are legions of angels waiting for the beck and call of the Master to have them strike when there is any need for it. This confused the Jewish leaders because what they were accustomed to is a physical kingdom, not a spiritual one.

Family, just like Jesus was not a part of this world, disengage from people who do not understanding your kingdom mind. You are not of this world when your thoughts line up with God's. Make it your lifelong pursuit to defend your kingdom. Values what has been put in you. Be willing to give up your life to ensure your kingdom is built on a firm foundation. That's where you need to be. That's what you need to take your love life to. That's where you need to dwell. You need sufficient knowledge of what His kingdom is and build your understanding around it. Understand that first. Separate yourself from people who are not sticking to this kingdom mindset.

You need to set yourself apart. Setting yourself apart means you are unwilling to compromise your hopes and dreams for someone else's happiness. Keep trying to have this mindset until you are focused on God's will. You need to lock into what your spirit has called you to do. You are being separated for His will and kingdom. Set yourself aside to do what He has called you to do—the mission He has for your life. Respond by aligning yourself to His transcendental will.

## Invest in the Kingdom

Having this kingdom mindset demands that you should invest in the kingdom mindset. The rich young ruler that questioned Jesus about making it to eternity did not understand this simple fact. He did not understand what the Father was trying to say to him when He told him "If you would be perfect, go, sell what you possess and give to the poor, and you will have treasure in heaven; and come, follow me" (Matthew 19: 21). The Father was trying to tell him, "Hey, I want you to invest in the kingdom or your purpose that builds others up."

You are a servant to why you were created—your mission. You are a tenant in this world, and He is the landlord. His Spirit is your helper. He is your friend, but most importantly, He seeks your sonship. He was saying to this young man, "I'll call you son and you'll call me Father." Unfortunately, the rich and young ruler did not understand all of this.

You are a part of the kingdom, and according to the Bible, the Father calls you into sonship. Yes, He wants you to be Christlike, but He calls you his child, His son or daughter. You are a part of the kingdom family. You are royalty. You are a prince or a princess, a king and a priest, and that's what your Father calls you.

Understand the Father's will and His intention when He said, " I will be a father to you, and you shall be sons and daughters to me" (2 Corinthians 6: 18). Do you understand this? What is true kingdom mindedness about? This is a spiritual step that's a part of your life. It's about the kingdom. Everyone who connects to His kingdom looks different.

Desire to be like Zacchaeus who was identified as the one on the sycamore tree who had the Master for dinner. Identifying with the kingdom means you have to take up this mantle He has given you, and most importantly, lift your standards and thoughts and let the King of Glory fight your battles for you.

God leads you and you lead and serve others. Apply the correct principles over your life based on what the Word of God has spoken about you. One of the purposes of His

Word is to make your relationship with Him better. The Word is truth and He says you are not a mistake.

Follow the instructions Jesus has left for you—words that have been in place since the beginning. He's is the Alpha and the Omega, the beginning and end of it all. What should give you peace of mind is that your life is in the Word of God and His leadership makes you understand what leadership is all about.

According to Webster, leadership is an action word.

- The act of leading a group of people or an organization
- The art of motivating an individual toward a goal
- Giving direction on what to do

Trust God to lead you well. Obey everything he says to do, and if He puts you in the role of leader, you will have the best role model you could ever hope to follow in Him.

# — 6 —

# BE SELFISH ABOUT FILLING YOUR INNER CIRCLE

*"A man of many companions may come to ruin, but there is a friend who sticks closer than a brother."*
*—Proverbs 18:24*

I came up with a philosophy that other people had to earn the right to have a seat at my table. Only individuals who understood my value were given the opportunity to come into my inner circle.

Being single does not define who you are, but it does give you time to step up and take control of your life before you're not single anymore. Trust and accept the process and God's timing on this. Believe that you have been placed among people who understand your value, and if they don't, create a new space where people do.

I've found that people operating from an unhealthy space tend to settle with people, letting them occupy their inner circle on a permanent basis instead of placing them first in their outer circle on a temporary basis to see if they pass the test. By allowing this to happen, they then subconsciously plant the roots for continuous heartache. Learn how to choose healthy friends before you go looking for a potential spouse. This is where you learn to get it right.

You have to understand how to get out of an unhealthy space and handle uncomfortable situations today. If you learn how to protect yourself from making bad decisions now, you'll be able to stay in a long and mutually healthy relationship later. Timing is everything, and the healthier you become, the more you can live as an independent thinker.

As an independent thinker, you only allow things to enter your inner circle after they've gone through a screening process you've created, one which removes the weaknesses that are not beneficial to your life. This can only happen when you believe that you are too valuable to get entangled with anything or anyone who has an issue with who you are.

## A Healthy Environment

I might speak of a healthy environment, but it's up to you who you choose to include in yours and in what capacity they will function, or by how much space they will take on. Put your cautious eyes on and regard everyone with the mindset that you are only out to build your personal healthy environment. It's essential to your growth that you take on the full responsibility of your choices, and when you get a lot of practice in this area, you start making wiser choices regarding who you want to be in an exclusive environment with.

Choosing an inner circle of friends who will bring you peace should be your priority. Carefully vet everyone trying to take up space in your life. Don't let any junk in. When you've created the space you want and are content in it, you'll find it easier to focus on your personal development and embrace the process.

Being recognized as a friend is earned and should not be taken lightly. Friendship is a mutual agreement between two people who come together and establish a respectful bond. You appreciate each other and the bond you have, and you don't disrespect the connection. You hold your friend in high regard. After listening to people provide me with their definition of a friend, I believe a lot misunderstand what a friend really is.

## The Associate

In a lot of cases, people have incorrectly defined an associate as a friend. It is vital to your growth that you realize that an associate is not a friend, nor should you treat a friend as an associate. An associate is someone you should keep at a distance, ridding them of the possibility of inflicting pain in your life. At times, some people make the mistake of trusting an associate as they would a friend. An associate belongs in your outer circle.

Everyone you have built a friendship might have started out as an associate, but not everyone stays in that position. There is nothing wrong with being an associate. This person is in your life for a specific purpose, a particular period, and usually stays in a specific location. They often provide resources that help make your life better.

An associate has withstood the test of time, but that friendhsip is connected to a shorter timetable. Your goal is to extract everything you can from this individual within that timeframe. What is interesting about an associate is that they know what their job is. I have seen a lot of people allowing an associate to get comfortable in their inner circle—a space not designed for them. Two people are impacted by that: the incorrectly placed associate and the person the position was designed for. To be effective, it is your responsibility to ensure that you vet people properly before positioning them in your inner circle.

## Being a Friend

Being called a friend should be earned over a period of time. If you are identified as a friend, it means you have endured the test of time. You've gone through some things together, and you are comfortable letting your guard down. When you understand the true meaning of what a friend is, you will realize that their proper placement in your life is key to your sufficient growth.

Friendship is an interpersonal bond. You stay linked together, and you promise to protect one another from harm. You are not afraid to give away something you value to a friend. This friend is a person who can receive what you have to give and appreciate what you have already built. You can trust that the friendship will not be taken out of context. Your heart is in the right place, keeping your friend in a proper perspective. If your friend says something to you that you view as hurtful, you are mature enough to have a conversation with them about how their words affected you. This conversation is not about establishing who's right or wrong because it stems from the goal of keeping the connection strong and valuing it. You don't allow any misunderstanding to fester. You are bonded, and that connection is created to last for eternity.

When I'm in a friendship, I can trust that what I give to my friend will not be exposed to anyone else, and my friend believes that what I have obtained from them has been put in a sacred place. Once you realize this about friendship, you relax and enjoy it.

Know when you are a friend and not an associate and fill that role well. When you know and accept your position, you can avoid the pressure of trying to be something you are not. Your goal within your space/circle (or in someone else's space) is to remove any obligation a person may feel in developing a friendship with you. You want to allow them to operate in an area that will enable them to be who they are. Being the person they have identified you as removes expectations on both sides, and you won't be viewed as fake.

You want to be with people who are genuine and pure. As my friend, when you are operating in your purest form, the information I receive from you is going to be beneficial to my growth. As my associate, I have to be cautious about what I receive from you. Too many people have destroyed their lives by not valuing the importance of placing friends and associates in their inner circle and outer circle correctly.

It is okay to be honest with yourself and accept that not everyone is going to be your friend. Nevertheless, you have to make sure you are friendly to the ones you have identified as your friends. If you're friendly, you have learned how to treat people effectively. If you don't know how to welcome someone, it makes it difficult to even establish a friendship, let alone recognize the importance of friendship.

## The Importance of Friendship

First and foremost, you should determine what it means to be a friend—you stick together all the way to the end like Frick and Frack—two people so closely associated as to be indistinguishable. You act like your friendship has value and you both matter. Your friendship is like a forcefield that pulls you both along. You share an unbreakable bond—nothing can separate you from one another.

As a friend, you have to enjoy being around one another. You accept your own authenticity and your brother or sister's. Building a strong brother or sisterhood with someone can at times can cause problems between siblings because you prefer your friend's company to your siblings'. Just like anything worth having, you have to invest time and energy into making your friendship what you desire it to be. Siblings should not get upset over things they do not view as valuable, including spending time with you. The beautiful thing about being a friend is that both parties invest time in one another, and the return on investment is more significant than the initial investment.

So based on how you've spent your time on the friendship, would it seem to an outsider that you think your friendship is a good investment? Does it look like you value your friendship? It should be worthy of your time. In the same way, being a friend worthy of another's time means you appreciate the time you spend together.

## Recognize a Friend

There are several things I believe are essential in recognizing a friend.

### Does the other person possess the right qualifications to be identified as your friend?

That's the first thing you should ask. Do a screening process to determine who they are. If you have no standards for choosing your friends, then you have no value for the friendship. A friendship should be governed by mutual respect, and some things have to be predetermined before you grant the other person access to your sacred space.

Friendship is like getting your driver's license. In order to be able to drive on the highway, you have to pass a test that determines your worthiness. Upon passing the test, you are given the authority to drive on the highway. There's a process you go through before you get your driver's license, and I think it's sad that people make more effort to get their driver's license than they do with their choice of friends for life.

Friends learn how to build trust with each other, they learn to trust that the information a friend gives will not harm them. Associates don't know how to handle certain data entrusted to them and, being immature, they often use the information to their advantage. A true friend will guard the information with their life because they understand the value of what has been given to them. When choosing friends to make yourself vulnerable to, I encourage you to use wisdom. Information in the wrong hands can be detrimental to your development.

When you want a healthy connection, you want friends who genuinely care for you enough to keep your private information safe. I often joke about how my sister Sharron chose the wrong career path. She should have been an attorney or an FBI agent, considering she's famous for safeguarding secrets. This is what you should want in a friend—the safety of knowing they won't place you in a position where your heart could be compromised.

When you are at peace with yourself, you don't feel the need to try to change a person into someone you desire them to be just so you can make your own life more comfortable. You are someone who takes what's before you at face value. When you receive your friends for who they are, you become even more comfortable in being the person God created you to be. When you don't accept a person "as-is," they can't trust you to be authentic and won't see you as a friend because you have an agenda.

Make sure that what a person presents to you is something you have validated as being okay to receive—what they talk about, their attitude, how they handle responsibility, their choices, etc. You want to receive what a friend has to give when it's beneficial to your development. Understand your worth. Only share and receive information that comes from a trusted source. As a friend, you have been vetted too, so check that what you have to give is solid and that your friends can depend on you for truth.

When it comes to associates, you have to position them appropriately in order not to allow them to abuse the relationship. When done wisely, associates properly positioned cannot cause any harm to you. Damage only takes effect if you turn them into a friend without their earning the rights to the position.

## Being a Leader over Others

When you are in a position of leadership, most of those working with you will be associates rather than friends. Seek understanding about the authority God has given you, and understand it is only given so that you will reign over things and not individuals. God is the one who reserves the right to dominate individuals and provide them with guidance in and understanding of their purpose. When you know the purpose of the seeds of greatness God planted in you, you have all His power and authority backing you up as you develop them.

The Bible contains all the necessary instructions to build you up to do the things you have been created to do, and the Holy Spirit provides all the power you need. I encourage you to take ownership of God's power instead of trying to manufacture your own. It comes from the One who understands you better than anyone. So be inspired to do everything heaven requires of you. You are a vital link in God's network of helpers, and you can help so many others accomplish their goals besides your own.

As a leader, it is important that you comprehend what being in a position of power entails. You use your power in a way that causes others to naturally respect you. If you lead effectively, your consistency will make things happen. The calling upon your life means you should pursue your purpose more than get caught up with being in a leadership position because purpose tells you *why* you should live out your calling.

Growing in a leadership role and finding balance in it is like cooking a meal. First, you have to wash, measure, peel, and dice up all the ingredients, and then you throw it in the pan. It takes some preparation to make a good meal. Give yourself grace as you figure it out with God.

# — 7 —

# BE SELFISH ABOUT WHO YOU DATE

*Then the anger of the Lord would be kindled against you, and he would destroy you quickly.*
*– Deuteronomy 7:13*

As a single person, you need to learn how to create, choose, and operate in a healthy space before you ever think of dating. Your relationship-building plan should be to only connect with people who respect your space. Never question that your present state of being single is a mistake. Being single does not mean you are alone or that you're somehow "lesser than."

When you swap out your expectations for God's, you lose your self-doubt and choose to operate in an area built on excellence. You're no longer desperate to find value in yourself; you're free. And by living a free life, you show you have chosen not to be that person who walks upon the earth as someone desperate. Desperate people tend to be like the zombies in *The Walking Dead*—they lack understanding and are unable to identify with reality. Operating in this realm of self-doubt will cause you to lose faith in the One who has created and given you life. God is the one who has the power to restore your life. He left His spirit to remind you that you are a uniquely constructed individual and that through wisdom, you will learn how to function in greatness. You are not an accident! You are not a mistake! You are amazing!

God created you and you are someone marvelous, therefore you only have time to get involved with people who will help you grow and expand your life, including those you date. Implementing the right things moves your life to the next level, and because you are single, you can take advantage of the time made available to you to do this. Don't put your life on pause waiting for the right person to appear. Life cannot stop and wait for that desire to be fulfilled; you have to keep moving forward, so be a mature person and live your life zealously and to its maximum capacity.

There is a misconception in the church about being single that implies you fare better in life when you are in a relationship. Ladies and gentlemen, I am here to let you know that the best place to be is a place that allows you to operate in peace. God is the one who creates an atmosphere of peace (John 14:27). I encourage you to be satisfied with your single status. In the Bible, everything that God has established was created from a single-status position. When you have learned to stand by yourself, it makes it easier to stand next to someone else. Accepting the way God created you is a prerequisite to amplifying your own greatness. I encourage you to shed any lingering regrets about your attractiveness and your singleness. God gave you the authority to live from a mindset of being victorious and to create the space you want to live in. Work from your place of dominion.

The Word of God teaches that it's in your best interest to be single but to be ready to transition when the timing is right. To be able to transition effectively when that opportunity comes, you'll never again settle with whatever you can get because you are set on God's best.

## The Three Ships

As you learn how to bond with people in a healthy way, you'll understand the three *ships* and how they play a significant but different role in a single person's life:

1. *Friendship*
2. *Dating relationship*
3. *Courtship*

The common denominator on these three is that they're *ships* and, therefore, structured not only to carry you to your destination, but also to protect you along the way.

## Dating Relationship

A dating relationship should be built on a firm foundation of friendship. When you no longer only want the other person as a friend but as someone you can go to the next level with, you are looking for a dating relationship with them.

Having started out with a friendship, you've done the preparation work needed to enter a healthy relationship, and you have strengthened your relationship with God to where you know He is bringing you together. By having Him as your center, you both hear Him clearly and share that level of understanding about the Lord with each other. You are ready to plunge into the relationship with all this, along with an inpouring of energy that makes you feel you are built for this, but you must anchor yourself in God's appropriate resources so you will operate in a way that benefits your connection. This can be challenging.

Being challenged sharpens your ability to focus on the finer things in life. Sharpening the skills of growing a relationship helps you to mature in how you speak, what you say, when you say it. It is essential to your growth that you understand the difference between speaking life or death. Simply put, your words either improve a situation or destroy it. When you contribute to a healthy relationship, you craft your words to shift your world and make things happen for the better. When you recognize the true meaning of friendship and are a good friend, you are fully prepared for the investment dating takes. You comprehend the seriousness of the commitment. You already knew how to value the good things and discard the bad ones that pass you by, and in a dating relationship, there will be both.

Connect to and focus on the fruit of the relationship, and the seeds God has planted will yield fruit in your life. Trust in the God-given process—it comes from a source far bigger than you. Flee from the thoughts that gravitate toward fear. Fall in love with the understanding that God painted a picture of you that only you can replicate because you are the only person God has given it to. He is a good God. You are a unique person who has evolved over time. You follow the footprints of the One who desires you to prosper.

Successful people understand that they couldn't have gotten there on their own. They are successful because of the exceptional people they allowed in their lives. It is up to you to only date an individual who is appropriately wired to God's growth plans. One of the main goals of your relationship is that you learn how to enjoy one another in peace and harmony.

## Stay Exclusive

A healthy relationship must be established as an exclusive experience. This should be positioned at the beginning of the relationship—where the foundation of the relationship is laid. The connection you already share with your friend can then produce hope, deeper trust, and a deeper connection.

A solid foundation can support any impact. The relationship is built on it, and trust helps you establish a healthy relationship. It contains wisdom from the things you learn in all three phases of friendship, courtship, and now a relationship. I find it interesting that some people believe a relationship can be established over a short period. I am not saying it is not possible, but if you are planning to be vulnerable with someone, it should be a person who has earned your trust.

You need to envision a relationship of trust. Think of it like cooking a meal in a crockpot—the spices go through a slow process of bringing the ingredients together as they are cooked, which is the key to making the food taste good. Once trust has been added to the equation, you know how to build a truthful and meaningful relationship. There is nothing like the feeling you get when you are with someone you trust. That takes time.

## Communication while Dating

If you stop seeing the person you are in a relationship with as a friend, you could push him or her away emotionally, triggering unhappy memories from other relationships where trust was not present. If you don't learn how to get past the situation and restore trust, you will allow the pain to be the driving force that pushes that person away. Getting past a situation like this requires communication where you are willing to express your thoughts honestly, without being offensive. Healthy communication has to be the basis of how you will learn and grow together. Expressing my honest thoughts means I respect you enough to not only tell you how I feel, but to allow you to express your feelings too.

## Being Misunderstood

Understanding a person and communicate with them in a healthy way will prevent you from jumping into an emotions-driven relationship. Through years of experience, you learn to keep your emotions in check rather than let them lead the way. People governed by their feelings lack balance and eventually end up in bad situations. You must get your emotions under control to be able to place people in the appropriate category in your space.

When you meet someone for the first time, vet them carefully before making them your exclusive friend (aka boyfriend or girlfriend). Perceive yourself as a person of *quality* rather than *quantity.* When a person has respect for you, they are willing to be vetted. They understand the value of the relationship and—most importantly—how valuable time is. Make them earn their title.

There's nothing like being with someone nice you can communicate with in a healthy way. It makes you hopeful that a time will come when you will flow together from a position of understanding. You want to know the type of person you are involved with, so it's okay to have standards in the relationship. The way I see it, it should be required before even thinking of going any further.

## Dating Rules

Having rules does not mean a person should assume certain expectations will be met. The relationship requirements should be communicated upfront to prevent any misunderstandings. You should let them know which things you are willing to deal with and which not. This way you establish your boundaries early on and give them the option of agreeing or not. You have to bear in mind, though, that this is a mature conversation between two people of the same mindset.

In a relationship, choose someone whose thoughts are peaceful and good. This is an invaluable person, an asset, and you'll notice things about them make you rejoice over what you have found. On the other hand, if you prematurely put a friend in a relationship, you put yourself at risk and make the connection difficult.

Never choose to be with anyone or anything you don't find beneficial. I believe things that are not beneficial should be viewed as evil because if it's not beneficial, it's detrimental to your growth. People with destructive intentions will seek you out. They are undisciplined and walk around with a reprobate mind. They believe the implementation of healthy principles is a waste of time.

A wise person understands that godly principles serve as the foundation for your behavior. It's going to take time to filter out things that are not needed to walk right, just like it takes time for a baby to mature and become an adult. It is going to take time for you to understand what's good and what's not right for you. I encourage you not to rush things. Sharpen your mind by reading books or find a mentor, but—most importantly—come up with a personal plan of action that will hold you accountable to living life according to these principles. Taking ownership over the things you are responsible for makes it okay to go back to the drawing board to make the appropriate adjustment when you feel off balance.

It baffles me when I hear people complaining about a relationship they have chosen to be in for many years. I believe people possess the ability to obtain wisdom through life experiences. You decide to be with someone who does not appreciate you. Accept the fact that it is your fault for refusing to change and choosing to be with an unhealthy person. The life you lead is in your hands to control. If you are dating a person like this, dare to move on. You have to work hard to be in a fulfilling relationship.

A fulfilling dating relationship means you have put the right person in the place. You are committed. They can trust you. You can trust them. You mutually respect each other. You have chosen to be content with each other. If you are willing to be that person and so are they, then you can move forward with that individual. Your future is based on how well you meet the needs of others, including your future spouse. Do you believe the relationship possesses the energy to keep you connected for life?

## Foundation for a Relationship

Commitment shows you support your decision to be together. If the relationship is going to be stable, you are required to go after the deeper things that anchor it. Dig deep—you are searching for information that will let you know if it is worth your time to move forward. Not investing in the foundation can cause your relationship structure to crumble and fall.

Invest your time in someone who has the willingness to do the hard work of understanding, learning communication, and bringing peace. This proves they value the relationship as much as you do and helps you understand the direction of the relationship. It allows you to control the force behind the relationship.

## Don't Be Afraid to Ask the Tough Questions

You are valuable. The purpose of asking questions before you get into a relationship is to know what you can benefit from vs what might cause your growth to regress. It's all about being an adult. You should not shy away from asking questions that make them uncomfortable. *The deep calls to deep*, and you are diving for information because you are unwilling to jack your life up for the benefit of someone else.

I believe it's essential you know at least the following:

- Look into their history.
- Look into prior relationships.
- Look at how they conduct themselves around loved ones.
- Who do they surround themselves with?
- Who are the people they look up to?

- What are their aspirations?
- How do they manage their finances?

It's essential to know the person you plan to invest a significant amount of time in.

## Getting to Know the Family

When you are getting to know a person, getting to know the family is a critical component because they are a reflection of the person you are inquiring about. You want to look at every aspect of their life that played a role in their development. Yes, I know that as an individual, they have the capacity of thinking for themselves; nevertheless, there are things you can learn if you understand the foundation they were built on. It's essential to see how they interact with their family and everybody who played a part in their upbringing.

You need to allow this person to operate in a space they are comfortable with. If you see something you don't like, voice your concerns and allow them to tell their side of the story. The best way to address a situation is by accepting there are three sides to a story. You have one person's side of the story, then you have the other person's side of the story, then you have the truth. The thing about truth is that it doesn't take sides as it is based on facts. But it's important to know the truth and believe in it.

You have to be with someone standing on a solid foundation themself to be able to see things for what they are. Being single does not mean that either of you is alone. You're not even lonely. You're already complete and don't need anybody except God. In wanting to date, you've both decided that you might make a good team together.

You have to carefully vet every person who approaches you. You have to make them earn the right to be on your team. You have to be able to see a future with them filled with joy, but you have to also be with someone who desires to be with you.

The other person has to be able to equip him or herself to be in a relationship with you because if they're not equipped, they are not prepared for being a relationship with you or anyone else. They would take you for granted and wouldn't be able to discover your full potential or the value of commitment. But if you are willing to be honest and upfront with them before a relationship even starts, then you can experience a dating relationship full of joy.

# — 8 —

# BE SELFISH ABOUT WHO YOU COURT

*But I found none.*
*– James 1:17*

This is the part of your life where all the boxes have been ticked and you are ready to bet it all on the other person being "the one." Asking and giving your hand in marriage means you are clear about where you would like to go. Both individuals are prepared to step into a place they have never been before.

This next phase in your life starts the process of you guys coming together as one. In oneness, you understand you are with someone who grew up looking at life in a completely different light than you. Your goal is to find ways to work through situations together. This is one of the things couples seem to struggle with.

But if you don't give up, you will find a system that works for you, and coming to a place of agreement will become easier. When you are in accordance with the other person, you can see yourself having a future with them, and when that happens, you find you keep investing in something bigger and better than you.

Courtship is something that happens over time. Before you proceed into a marriage, ensure that you are being honest with yourself. You need to make sure you do not have any concerns about who you are getting yourself involved with. Ensure you are satisfied with the leap you are about to take. I have learned that a lot of people transition but aren't ready to transform into a marriage that's supposed to be held in high honor.

Even when you are engaged, you need to be willing to let go of the person if neither one of you transforms the way you're supposed to. Transformation proves each of you has the commitment needed to make a marriage work. If it's not present during the engagement, it sure won't be present in the marriage. As a responsible adult, remember not to be immature in making a decision. Analyze your situation from the position of building something together forever with the person you are planning to spend the rest of your life with.

If you find an issue that concerns you, don't be afraid to address it. If you refuse to do so, you will experience issues once you get settled in. Address the issues at an appropriate time and you will be able to build something special, based on trust. A structure built on trust can withstand the weight and pressures of life.

## Security in your Relationship

Security is defined within yourself first. It's not based on anything but you and God. You appreciate your strengths and you flow with God and His plans for your life. You are in a good place. Once this person is in your life, you can then appreciate their place in your inner circle, only now the space belongs to both of you. Do you feel safe having them there? Do they feel safe being there? When that person is someone I appreciate having in my space, I am willing to do everything there is to move forward with this individual.

I'm going to give it my all. I'm willing to give up some things just to ensure I'm analyzing this thing correctly—that this person should be one with me for life. And when I say give up something, I'm referring to the time it takes to get to know that person properly before moving on to the next level.

Having gone through *friendship, relationship,* and now *courtship,* you need to understand when it is better to be together and when it is better to part ways. It's truly amazing when you are with someone who makes you better instead of bitter. That's a person you don't want to become and a place you need to avoid. You cannot grow with the individual who drives you into a sad place, and it's rather disappointing when it happens. It's not what you expected, and that leaves a nasty taste in your mouth. I'm sure a lot of you can relate to that.

Before you two become one, you start building a bond that will hold you together through good and bad times. The satisfaction that comes from this is a reward for investing in the courtship stage of the relationship. Early on, I decided to invest my time, energy, money, or whatever it took to ensure I built a firm foundation for my marriage. If you do these things, trust me, everything will work out just fine, even in disagreement. Understand the lack of investing means a lack of the resources that will allow you to receive certain benefits once married.

Don't sit idle, wishing to be with someone you can't be yourself around, someone who makes you concerned about your relationship. Be willing to let go of someone like that because sooner or later, you'll start to question yourself, and that's something you don't want to do.

There are a few points I would like you to consider during courtship. Establish what you are willing to do before contemplating marriage.

## God Brought You Two Together

That's the firm foundation you'll be building on. That is what it's really all about because God brought you two together. That means you guys have linked together at the appropriate time and appropriate place. The reason I mention this is because you have to understand that if the Father is going to have you walk together with someone, you have to trust God to link you up with someone who's going to be beneficial to your life. It's no accident that this person comes into your life. There's something about you that makes you stand out and vice versa.

There's something about the person that draws you to them. You can see your relationship and your future transitioning with him or her to courtship. You can see a future with them, and a bright one at that.

## THERE SHOULDN'T BE A DIMMER SWITCH

Connect with the wrong person and your life starts to turn downhill. This dimmer switch turns everything in the wrong direction. You have to ensure that your future stays bright and that you can see yourself being complete with that individual. You have to understand the path of improvement.

You should have certain expectations of this thing going to a beautiful place. It should move your life in a spectacular way. With the right person, you will be able to see yourself down the road in another place, another destination, but most importantly at another level. Do you understand that? With this person you are seeing yourself with is going to change the world and construct something beautiful.

Many people confuse happiness with joy, but they're two different things. Being happy doesn't mean you just enjoy being married. On the contrary, happiness is a constant thing acquired by companionship and trust, and it takes work. Joy is something God places inside you that you can access. It's not based on circumstances on relationships. Be with someone who has the firm foundation in the Lord so you can build something solid together powered by His joy.

# — 9 —

# BE SELFISH ABOUT DOING LIFE GOD'S WAY

*Again Jesus spoke to them in parables, saying, "The kingdom of heaven feast." – Matthew 22:2*

To be in a good place, it's your faith or commitment to having peace that motivates you not to be thrown off your game. God is our loving Father and the ultimate director of all our steps and activities. If we're to walk the highway of holiness with Him, He gives us what we need to walk in integrity, honesty, and humility and live within His boundaries when it comes to our behavior and speech.

We are servants to serve the Father, which is going set you apart from some people. You are different, but most importantly, you come here to serve—serve God and serve others. That's ultimately what Jesus was trying to teach us about being a part of the kingdom.

If I have a conversation with you, my job is to encourage you to get to a place where you believe in yourself. When you believe in yourself, you can encourage yourself to live life to the fullest.

Believe in the process, and now believe that your relationship with each person around you can get better. Believe it will continue to move in the correct direction for what's in your best interest because your mindset has already sent you in the right direction. But when you're beaten down, and you're going through tough things life throws in your direction, know the Lord will be there for you. When the Word of Truth has transformed your mind, you will do things differently.

> Continue in what you have learned and have firmly believed, knowing from whom you learned it and how from childhood you have been acquainted with the sacred writings, which are able to make you wise for salvation through faith in Christ Jesus. All Scripture is breathed out by God and profitable for teaching, for reproof, for correction, and for training in righteousness, that the man of God may be complete, equipped for every good work.
>
> —2 Timothy 3:14–17

Scripture is breathed out of God's mouth. Breathe in the Word so you can grow and mature. You have to be mature to receive His correction and apply His training in righteousness. You have to make sure you're ready to do this thing so that when you receive understanding about how to apply it to your life, you will use every last thing He teaches you to be His representative. He gives you clarity. As a representative of the One who is dependable, you will become dependable too. As you mature in your thoughts, you will notice the transformation. You'll fit into your purpose more clearly, and you'll be more Christlike. On the flip side, when you do something that does not line up with your purpose, your mindset will start changes to justify your actions. Never step outside His will. The cost is too great.

If you trust in Him, you can depend upon Him. When you place trust in a mortal man, he may slip and stumble because man, by default, does not have the requisite strength to sustain another human. No man died on the cross for you. Most men will readily renege on their words and promises because they are not sufficient for your needs. It is not entirely their fault because their nature does not permit them to carry more than they can bear. To not be heartbroken over broken trust, the best bet is to focus your mind on the One who promised to take upon Himself all your burdens and do something no one else would do—give you the rest your soul longs for.

Desire to be reproved and corrected, but most importantly, desire to look forward to being trained every day of your life. Applying something each day as you develop and move forward. He has done His part teaching you what you need to move your life forward; the onus is now on you. Make the necessary corrections in your life. God promised to transform your life if you give Him the opportunity to do so. You don't have to have all of the answers while starting, but you should also know you can go to Him and receive the answers you need. He is ever ready to listen to your demands and provide you with the answers you need.

Ensure you keep your flesh under subjection. Invest in improving your relationship with God and with the people around you. Invest in making your relationship with your significant other better. Make sure it is a reflection of something amazing. Do something with your relationship that causes other people to be encouraged with their lives. You may not know who you are saving.

The world is already filled with angry and frustrated people. Don't be a source of discouragement to someone else. You can enjoy your relationship with the world if you seek to put smiles on people's faces. Encourage and convince yourself of the truth that you are different from others. We have all heard people saying it is common for men to cheat. You'll want to rewrite this narrative if you want to be the best you can be. God's will and solutions are very different from what the world proposes as solutions. Society often suggests you do things are not in line with God's will. Only He provides healthy direction. As His son or daughter, your desire is to be in line with His will; as such, always strive to do the things according to His Word. The results will be positively reflected in your life.

Live from your spirit—the one where the Holy Spirit resides. Live as one with Him. Many things will consume you and try to distract you from what should have your attention, but the kingdom is about the spiritual things, not the tangible things your eyes can see and relate to. Don't get so caught up in things that cannot produce a spiritual profit. Know how to link up and tighten your core self with Him. When you communicate with your spirit via meditation on the Word, let it know life is not always about material things. It's about the spiritual, and God has many Spirit-filled elements He wants to fill your life with so you can then impart them to those around you.

You need to get away from those trying to pull you away from this kingdom mindset. Stay far from those people and don't let them attach themselves to you. Use your free will to dwell in the kingdom. Ask God to catch you and split you apart from those earth-minded people who try to entrap you.

To understanding how to separate yourself from people who are not dedicated to the kingdom mindset, read what the book of 2 Corinthians has to say.

> Do not be unequally yoked with unbelievers. For what partnership has righteousness with lawlessness? Or what fellowship has light with darkness? What accord has Christ with Belial? Or what portion does a believer share with an unbeliever? What agreement has the temple of God with idols? For we are the temple of the living God; as God said,
>
> "I will make my dwelling among them and walk among them,
>
> and I will be their God,
>
> and they shall be my people.
>
> Therefore go out from their midst,
>
> and be separate from them, says the Lord,
>
> and touch no unclean thing;

then I will welcome you,

and I will be a father to you,

and you shall be sons and daughters to me,

says the Lord Almighty."

—2 Corinthians 6: 14–18

The Father told you to separate yourself from the unclean things of the world. When you have this mindset, it will be reflected in your choices, proving how much value you have for yourself. Those things that make you unclean are opportunities you sign up for that show you are not living from the kingdom mindset God designed for you. The truth is the world will not understand what it means to be kingdom minded but you do. Hence, you need to separate yourself to stay in that mental space for life.

Accept that you have been created differently than anyone else and refuse to be "average." When you want to make your life different, you start by separating from people who are not "assets." The world is full of confused people looking for the validation of other people. Many people love being told, "You are sexy" or "You are beautiful." Make sure you do not fall into this trap of seeking the validation of other people, rather try to immerse yourself in His will.

God alone knows what is best for you, and so do you when you walk with Him. The validation of other people is certainly not what is best for you. It will not lead you to the future God has prepared for you.

What are you trying to attract in your life? That's the question. You have a different, unique to only you mission, so there is no duplicate elsewhere. Only you can fulfil your custom-made mission, and part of that includes attracting holiness, not people's validation. Dwelling in holiness mean you recognize you were created as an empty vessel only God fills—with knowledge and understanding about what's needed to fulfil your calling.

You don't need to agree with people who do not understand how to be in an effective relationship with you. Know your life has value. Don't be ashamed of disallowing negative lines of communication. Communicate your kingdom mindset to the world, and speak life over those who teach you and cause you to keep moving. Fall in love with knowing you were created to make an impact. Entrench yourself in being willing to do what you have to do to expand your life.

The relationship you have with your spirit requires that you not waste time in thinking about who is on your side.

## When Temptation Comes

You want to be secure in who you are. You want to be hinged on God's thoughts and actions and be known for your stable mindset. Be so trustworthy that people can look in your eyes and see what is to come. It's different to being someone who has a heart made of gold or who is perfect. You have obvious shortcomings, but people will know you as the resilient one who stands firm in truth no matter what anyone else around you wants to do. Temptations are bound to come, but if you have your moral and spiritual stamina already built in, you can easily escape the daunting effects of temptations, irrespective of the angles they are coming from.

Temptation reveals the parts of our lives we are struggling with. While the Enemy sends it to cause harm, we can turn it to our benefit when we seek to see the good side of it. For example, when we are tempted, we can easily redraw our boundaries past where we are likely to fall so we can sin, or we pull them even closer.

By knowing your area of weakness, you can easily seek the Lord to help strengthen that part of you. One good thing about the Lord we serve is that He will not allow anything to come to your direction if He has not provided you with the requisite strength to overcome it. The Holy Book has something to say about this. "Let anyone who thinks that he stands take heed lest he fall. No temptation has overtaken you that is not common to man. God is faithful, and he will not let you be tempted beyond your ability, but with the temptation he will also provide the way of escape, that you may be able to endure it" (1 Corinthians 10:12–13). When you faithfully lean into Him for strength, even the biggest mountains will become as small as a piece of rock lying in a valley. Yes, your faithfulness is the key to living a pleasing life to the Lord.

The temptation is the desire to do something, especially something that is morally and spiritually wrong and unwise. What is temptation versus a trial? Popular theology draws a thick line between these two. While both of them can be likened to a test, trials make you stronger. They build your faith in the Lord. On the other hand, temptations reek of negativity. They are primarily orchestrated by the evil one to pull down the children of God and hurt them.

Use wisdom. Reside in His presence so you won't stumble and fall. When you are in line with the ways and precepts of God, you understand that there are certain places you can go to and there are certain things you can no longer do—because you want to ensure the relationship you have with the Lord is still intact. When you do this, people will respect you because they'll see you as an honorable person. And you want to be someone who is respected, someone who has honor about what they say and what they do. Take courage and make sure you are a man or woman of integrity.

This lifestyle is very attractive to God. It does not matter who has this mindset of integrity; keeping laws will always guarantee the desired results are received. This lifestyle will help you defeat the Enemy, who comes to you only to steal, kill, and destroy. It doesn't matter what he attempts to do to you because you stand upright before God as a person of integrity, a person who adheres to God's ordinances and worships Him relentlessly at His holy temple. This is the lifestyle that wins. This is the lifestyle that is pleasing to God.

The Father is well pleased with everything you do and everything you say if you have this mindset. You represent the Most High God, the King of Kings, and the Lord of Lords. He created you, and you have to be pleasing to His eyes. You want to ensure your heavenly Father takes pleasure in saying "Yes, that's my child who stands upright before me and also before men."

# — 10 —

# BE SELFISH ABOUT YOUR INTEGRITY

*"Whoever walks in integrity walks securely, but he who makes his ways crooked will be found out."*
*—Proverbs 10:9*

In whatever type of relationship you find yourself in, it's your duty to be a person of integrity with godly standards. The Word says to walk in integrity. You don't need to rush to walk in integrity. You need to be patient. You have to be very calm. Do not be under any pressure. Be gentle and tolerant. Be accommodating and easygoing and, more importantly, have a mindset of someone who always tells the truth, irrespective of the prevailing circumstances.

There should be no occasion to be dishonest with people when you are a person of integrity.

In your Christian journey, it is important to have spiritual strongholds that are rooted in God. Make sure the Father has that hold on you if you don't want to have a spiritual stronghold connected to the Enemy. This hold has to be a very strong and unbreakable bond that bonds you and Him together so you can walk with integrity. You can stand upright before people and let them know who the Father is because of the bond's strength between the two of you.

This bond is akin to the bond a parent shares with his or her child. It is no wonder the Bible calls us the children of God. Even in the animal kingdom, the bond between a mother and her offspring is almost always unbreakable. A mother hen will look out for her chick any day and at any time. The same applies to God. He is willing to look out for us even when we don't seem to notice it.

In your walk in life, if you imbibe God's teachings and stay close to a life of integrity, God will always fight for your interests. By placing God at the center of everything, your life becomes built on the Spirit of God. Your life will sail in the correct direction the Father desires it to go in, even if it may seem like you're getting off on the wrong path at times. The Father, who promised to be there for anyone who casts their cares on him, will surely be there for you. He cares for you and wants to give you whatever you desire.

God is always in control because He is a God of integrity. And because He is a God of integrity, when you receive Him as your Lord and your Savior, you can stand upright like a person of integrity yourself. This word of the Lord applies to everybody. It applies very much to those who are married, as well as to you who are still single. And one great thing about this word of the Lord is that it applies indiscriminately to everyone as long as His ordinances and principles are kept.

When you are involved in things like business transactions, you must be a person of integrity. This saves you a lot of headaches. Only doing transactions with people who have a fear of the Lord will most likely spell success for you. Read the Scriptures, for they say your steps will be secured when you are a person of integrity (Proverbs 10:9).

The opposite is the case if you are a person who lacks integrity: instead of being directed by the Word of the Lord, your steps will flow with the tides and waves of life. The sure thing is that it wouldn't be long before you got into trouble. Be a person of integrity. This should be a quality your family and friends can beat their chest over.

There are three core things you should know about integrity.

## Be Honest

An honest person is a person of virtue who stands for the truth, irrespective of everyone else's stance. An honest person is not morally bankrupt. He or she has a heavy wall of moral principles built around them to make sure they do not easily yield to the temptations lurking around the corner. Stand upright. It's a state of mind that the spirit of God can help form in your life.

He formed you as a whole being. You are not divided. You are not separate. You were not pulled apart by God when He created you. He created you whole, but it is up to you to choose to be a person of integrity. Do not be swayed to the left or right when it comes to making decisions. Stand firm in your beliefs and give an honest and unbiased report in everything you do.

You must hold people accountable for what they say and what they do when they want to enter your space. When dealing with anyone, you want to make sure a person is a person of integrity. Do not trivialize this. If your friend says, "I will come to pick you up at seven o'clock," he or she should get busy sticking to their words if they are going to respect your time. The same goes for you too. Keep the promises you made to your friends. If anything can make your friendship stronger, it is the fact that you respect your friend enough to keep your word. In the real sense of it, becoming a person of integrity is about pleasing or being appreciated by the people around you. Still, it should also be about pleasing and representing the Most High in the best possible way—the way He recommended in the Scriptures.

When you stand up and speak, you should command the respect of everyone around because you speak with the confidence that comes with telling the truth. There certainly will be loopholes offered and distractions set on your path as a result of this commitment of yours, but the Lord has this to say:

> Keep your heart with all vigilance,
>
> for from it flow the springs of life.
>
> Put away from you crooked speech,
>
> and put devious talk far from you.
>
> Let your eyes look directly forward,
>
> and your gaze be straight before you.

> Ponder the path of your feet;
>
> then all your ways will be sure.
>
> Do not swerve to the right or to the left;
>
> turn your foot away from evil.
>
> —Proverbs 4:23–27

Your obedience to the Lord and His principles should be sacrosanct, and nothing should command your reverence more.

You want to be honest because it is the right thing to be. You can be trusted and relied upon. In a world where dishonesty is gradually becoming a norm, standing out as an honest person is one of the best things about relating with the outside world.

To ensure you remain honest, make sure you do not rush to undertake anything you are not very sure of. Take your time and do it very well, and if possible, ask questions because making a hasty decision can come with unintended consequences later on. Striving to protect your values will harbor the God-factor in your life. Choosing a healthy mindset cannot be stressed enough. You don't want to tarnish your image by doing a few wrong things. Be 100 percent honest. I can't stress this enough!

When you make the right choices, you'll always be that conqueror who attracts other worthy people into your life. You make good choices even when the temptation seems to be glaring at you because you value who you are, what you have, and what you possess. Be honest about communicating what you stand for with the rest of the world. Lift a standard and sanctify your conversation. Put a guard over your mouth so it will never cause someone to stumble and fall. We cannot dismiss the fact that life moves up and down, with periods when you feel strengthened and times when you think you cannot make it, but whatever you are facing in life, always know you can stand up after a fall.

Apologizing to the people you hurt when you gave in to temptation is also something you should learn to do. It is impossible to not offend the people we love every now and then, even as we strive for perfection. But when we do, the onus is on us to apologize and make amends for our wrongdoing.

## Establish Your Principles and Values

This is a fundamental truth for anyone who wants to live a useful life. Being a principled person comes with many responsibilities, and what makes us stick to these responsibilities is our values. Sticking to our values ensures we will progress in all areas of our lives, relationships included.

A lot of people have personal principles and values, but when you rely on biblical principles when setting yours, you are different from the rest of the world. These principles will set you free from the Enemy's hurdles and oppression because they are the truth. The truth sets free, hallelujah! Make sure you're applying the right principles to obtain the right results.

When you don't have any moral principles, you'll slip and fall for anything, so decide on yours and be a person who can stand with absolute integrity and do the right things, irrespective of the prevailing circumstances.

Sometimes, your pre-salvation lifestyle can be the challenge keeping you from living the life of your dreams.

Make sure you keep those annoying characters you acquired from your childhood quiet to avoid a conflict of interest when they all start giving their opinion. Everyone has a different upbringing and a different way of seeing and doing things, and we might think they are the only godly way God works in many ways and all of them could be godly. When we try to superimpose our ideals and fantasies on people who don't share them, it can often be a source of misunderstanding. Everyone's character is as different as their faces due to the unique interplay between their environment and genetics, so we have different characteristics and ways of reacting to circumstances and words spoken. When we can tolerate and celebrate other's differences and admire their strengths, we become bridge builders. We strengthen our bond with whoever we relate to. Strive to bridge the gap of all these differences with your close associates. Try keeping everything open when there is a need to.

Make a decision to have an ironclad relationship with the principles that will help you become successful. It does not matter that no one else may see your choices, but they will be able to tell that you are connected to something that's changing your life. What a happy relationship when you understand that you are a person who has value! There is something about this relationship that gets you excited and motivated to talk more about the process. Your connection with the Spirit of truth causes you to speak from what He shows you, even when things don't add up.

## Be an Incorruptible Person

Being incorruptible means you have taken time to build your boundaries, strong spiritual walls around yourself to guarantee you don't fall when temptations and trials come your way. Integrity and incorruptibility are almost synonymous, and they will ensure you stand firm in your beliefs and stance in life. The world around us is filled with different vices and elements that can easily corrupt us when we provide a fertile ground for them. But when you make your guard stronger with the Word of the Lord, even the strongest temptations will pass by you without causing you any measurable harm. The Word of the Lord has substance and is the basis for your incorrigibility.

Your spiritual makeup is more important than your natural makeup and what people see about you. Your spiritual composition and essence cannot be shaped or destroyed without your permission or the consent of God's spirit in you. Man or the Enemy cannot control them because your spiritual makeup comes from God, and you have given it back to Him. You have opened your spiritual heart to receive Him and do His biddings.

The Father should be glorified within you. It is your duty as a faithful steward to magnify the Lord's name by building the right relationships and making Him the center of it. Let Him be your focal point and let Him be your inspiration. Always make it a habit to praise Him with your mouth so your mind will not be corrupted by the evil one. The evil one cannot do that to you when you are a spiritual force field in tune with God's Word.

For your relationship with people to flourish, you also need to have the mindset of someone who understands. As older people know, understanding is what keeps a union strong. When you create an atmosphere that encourages people to tell you intimate details knowing that you won't pass judgment, you are just a step to enjoying the best a God-directed life offers. The world has a different story to tell, but the Word of the Lord stands sure and doesn't value the opinion of the world when it's not founded on His Word.

## Wrapping Up

1. Being an honest person cannot be stressed enough. This quality builds trust between you and people, making the trust you have with them wax stronger.
2. Have personal principles and values. This quality makes you different from the world's standard because you are founded in the Lord and His Word.
3. Be incorruptible—a product of the first two points. An honest person has personal principles and values that he or she stand for. You will not be blown off your feet by every wind of doctrine.

Make sure you strive to have these qualities. They are pleasing to God. They are also pleasing to humanity.

.

# — 11 —

# BE SELFISH ABOUT BUILDING THE RIGHT MINDSET

*May the God of your hope so fill you with all joy and peace in believing*
*– Romans 15:13*

I played basketball in high school. I was never intimidated by more skilled athletes. I was of the mindset that regardless of the skills someone else may have, I would have no problem challenging them. I was confident in who I was and what I could do.

Long ago, I committed to never letting my mindset be moved by the opinions of others. This allowed me to relax and be all that God had created me to be. Because of this, I became an integral part of my high school winning its first and only basketball championship. During the Hillcrest High School 1993 state championship game, we had established a large lead against Byrnes High School. In the second half of the game, Byrnes took the momentum and cut the insurmountable lead down to a single digit. My coach, James Smith, yelled out, "Can anyone stop this guy?" I responded to my coach, "Put me in the game, coach; I can stop him." He looked at me and said, "Get in the game then." I entered the game, they passed the ball to their best player, and I stole the ball from him. I drove to the other end to the court and got foul by the opposing team. That steal changed the momentum and assisted in us in winning the game—because I had the mindset that I could do it and I spoke up at the appropriate time. This helped me understand the importance of understanding your role and having confidence in your abilities. If you don't have confidence in what you are capable of doing, who will?

Because what comes out of your mouth comes straight from your mind, God wants you to build the right mindset so your words aren't destructive. "The good person out of the good treasure of his heart produces good, and the evil person out of his evil treasure produces evil, for out of the abundance of the heart his mouth speaks" (Luke 6:45).

When you have heaven's mindset and have locked your thoughts on a specific target, you can improve and get better. Your life can be whatever you think it can be. When you are unwilling to be distracted, you'll perceive all relationships differently from how the world views them. Irrespective of the prevailing circumstances, the validity of *who* you are cannot be questioned. For anything to work in your life, you must validate *you* for yourself. Don't wait for anybody to do this for you.

Picture this. Picture yourself driving to a public space and you need to pay for a ticket to validate that you have the right to park your car there. Without that ticket, there is no way you can park your car. The Word, which operate as "truth," functions in the same way as the ticket. It can give validity to any area of your life that requires it, but you must engage it from your own end.

When Jesus Christ died on the cross, He validated your all-access pass to go out into the world. When you receive Him as your Lord and your Savior, He gives you access to understand His word. You'll do this through the Holy Spirit, who develops and grows the Word of God within you and inspires you to "go into all the world and proclaim the gospel to the whole creation" (Mark 16:15). When you receive Him, He validates your place in the world, gives you your mission, and fills you with purpose. He said, " The Spirit of the Lord God is upon [you], because the Lord has anointed [you] to bring good news to the poor; he has sent [you] to bind up the brokenhearted, to proclaim liberty to the captives, and the opening of the prison to those who are bound" Isaiah 61:6). People tell me all the time that they don't know what their purpose is, what God has called them to do. When you stay in the fight for the right mindset, you spend time with the Word of God. I have no doubts that you will find your purpose there.

Your mindset is what builds or destroys relationships. It controls the way you think about yourself, about your life, and, most importantly, about your relationship with the individuals you deal with. It controls what gets you motivated and discouraged about being in a relationship with that individual in the first place.

Your mindset also reflects what these individuals do to you or invest in your life. Whatever you believe within your heart causes you to move in certain directions in your relationship. If you're dealing with a bad situation, your mind starts to communicate with your spirit—mind, will, and emotions—when dealing with your heart. Your mind tends to speak to your heart, and then you believe what it tells you. That's why "confess with your mouth and believe in your heart" is essential to your growth. Your confession is to deal with the people on the earth, but your heart belongs to the One who created you. To put it better, your heart belongs to the person you give your heart to—one who is for you or against you. That person wants to get access to your heart to fill it with the right or wrong mindset, so fill it with God's truth first so you will not be swayed if that person is against you.

You'll say, "Okay, this is what I believe, and this is what I stand for, and this is the basis for my actions and beliefs. I believe and stand for it with all of my heart." When you know and believe what you think, it doesn't matter what anybody else says to you. For instance, no one can come to me and tell me that Jesus Christ isn't my Lord and my Savior. It is already my reality because it's in my heart. It's what I believe. I believe this in the core of my heart, the depth of my being that He's my Lord and my Savior, and no one can come and tell me otherwise. When they speak something else that's not true, I'll say, "I won't listen to what you're saying to me because it doesn't speak to my heart."

My heart has been covered by the blood of the Lamb that was slain on the cross of Calvary. Investing in this thing called the Word of God will transform the way your mind thinks. I communicate the way I do because I believe in my heart that if I speak what I believe is true, I can be transformed.

*Set your minds on things that are above, not on things that are on earth.*
*—Colossians 3:2*

"Mindset" is defined as the establishment of a set of attitudes. Family, you must have a practical approach to a mindset that positively identifies you because you will be identified based on what you believe in and live out, and what you believe in is intimately connected to your attitude.

The truth is that everyone has a set of attitudes reinforced by their mindset, and this reinforcement will either be negative or positive. This means you can get encouraged about your kingdom mindset. Get excited about who you are and don't run away from expressing your thoughts. It's like I said, when you encourage people that their relationship can get stronger, their whole attitude changes. I love my wife. We are always laughing and joking, and we look at each other in a special way because of the type of attitude we have towards one another. Getting there is a process that requires time. We are so thankful for what has developed in our relationship so far because we are willing to adjust and learn. It doesn't make us perfect; we are imperfect but we are eager to be developed. Anchor yourself in a mindset of excellence and get ready to be molded by Him into the shape and form He desires for your life. Be willing and eager to go through these things. Desire to be all God has called you to be based on you being willing to be taught.

## The Right Mindset Makes Relationships Strong

You can have a productive relationship with your coworkers because you have the right mindset. You can be useful in your job because the greater One lives inside you and there's nothing that you cannot accomplish.

God deals with your mind by connecting it to your heart. When you do something that does not line up with your purpose, the Spirit deals with your intention and He will reposition you back in line with the biblical principles that protect your life. This is an amazing thing about having the right kind of spirit. The Holy Spirit's job is to reveal things to you that He won't disclose to anyone else. His dealings with you are unique only to you. This is why imitating other people is futile—because everyone's dealings are unique to them.

Be thankful for all the people He has placed in your life. Obtain as much wisdom and understanding as you possibly can obtain from being around them. Be a person who is open to hearing and receiving the correct information so you can be built up with the correct mindset. The Word of God has been imparted into your life to give you spiritual harmony that will allow you to go help somebody else. The Spirit of empowerment quickens your spirit to hear what a trusted agent can teach you.

If you are willing to do these things, your life will become something that blows your mind. I have three points I believe will be beneficial for your relationship, and I pray you can apply these things. If you apply them to help your mind focus on your relationship, then you know it is only a matter of time before things will get better. You will become a more effective person than you used to be. Your mind is a battleground with a lot of forces contending for domination. It is a battle of getting your mind under control. Understand having a mindset with the correct perspective and your life will drastically change, like day and night. The things you want to change in your life will change because you have learned how to convince yourself to believe it will. When you convince yourself, trust me, your life will be headed in the right direction. The spirit of God is the life force that can help you effectively reinforce your mind for positivity.

## How Do You Perceive Your Relationship with People?

Your perception of your relationship is critical—what you believe and think about it and about how it should be—because it affects how you go about doing things that concern it. For example, God's Word tells you to train up a child in the way he or she should go, and they will not depart from it when they get old. A child is trained based on the context of how their parents or guardians understand relationships and, dictates how the children will interact with their environment. When a mother finds her child in an awful place, her initial reaction is usually, "What are you doing here?" or when she sees him doing things that displease her, she'll tend to say, "I didn't teach you those things. I didn't train you up in that way. So why are you conducting yourself in that way?" Just like the way your parents model how to do life, your relationship with your purpose will lead and direct your life.

You need wholesome relationships with people who can train you how to make your life more fulfilling. The relationships you choose to build should be based on your desire for connection to someone who understands you and you understand them. Be willing to be trained in your relationships with people every day if you want them to get better. You'll learn how to perceive your interactions with people and your expectations of the people you are close to. You'll learn how to talk with them in a healthy way.

You're always learning to order your mindset rightly. Make sure you are not conforming in the way the world thinks you should conform. Be transformed by the renewal of your mind as your spirit corrects your course every single day. Do things every single day that make your relationship with people better. Every time an acquaintance of yours is having a rough time with the things of this world, be transformed to respond in love.

When you know what you expect from your people, you're going to invest in them to make sure you reap happiness afterward. You are going to be doing things the kingdom way, the way the world thinks isn't a proper way of doing them, but their way doesn't matter. You do those things God's way because your mind has been transformed. You perceive everything and everyone differently. "Do not be conformed to this world, but be transformed by the renewal of your mind, that by testing you may discern what is the will of God, what is good and acceptable and perfect" (Romans 12:2). Your relationship with people in God's sight is good and fair, and it is His will that you make something good with your life. I want to assure you that your life is acceptable to him. That's why you should conduct yourself in the way the Word of Truth says, looking to improve yourself and get better every single day.

## The World's Way or God's Way

When you start doing things the way the world recommends, there's no light behind it. You will not enjoy a smooth ride as the relationship grows, plus you will start accepting and believing things that are clearly outside of what the Word of God says about you.

As a man or woman, at times you'll come across friends who are out to persuade you to do things that you know will offend the people you cherish. You'll hear them say things like, "It's alright to do those things." They will unknowingly encourage you to do things that are designed to destroy your life, because all they know about is ordinary relationships. It may be the norm in society, but do you have to do those things because your friends advised you to? No, family. You need to continuously incline your ears toward the Word that speaks truth to you. This is a tug of war. The enemy is after your heart, so when you understand what you are capable of with God, you cannot be overcome by the evil one, the Devil. We give the Devil too much credit sometimes. Yes, he's out there. He's out to get your mind to think about things outside of what God wants you to believe and focus on.

When you yield to the thoughts of the Enemy, you'll discover that you start communicating differently. Your speech will be more negative and so will your thoughts. Eventually your words and thoughts will manifest to destroy what God has planned out for your life. It's critical that you apply His wisdom to everything, and you can't do that if you are listening to the Enemy instead of the Word of Truth.

# — 12 —

# BE SELFISH ABOUT WATCHING YOUR MOUTH

*The righteous cry, and the Lord hears, and delivers them out of all their troubles.*

*– Psalm 34:17*

What are you saying? How you say things is very important. There's a difference in saying, "You are important to me" in a casual way and saying the same thing in an emotion-filled tone. You may truly consider that person you say this to plays a very important part in your life, but the way you say it goes a long way as to how the person will accept it. Do not attempt to take it casually because it may mean something great to that person. If you are facing a distance barrier with a person you truly miss, uttering such statements in the most affectionate way you can will help you bond with them more, plus it can also be a way of encouraging them and making them trust you.

You're fooling yourself if you don't think your speech matters. It's seen as a thermometer that indicates your level of affection for a person. A speech filled with warmness is an indicator of a smooth-running relationship. A cold speech when communicating with someone is the indicator of the exact opposite. It shows a lack of friendliness. Protect what you say and how you say it to be more than an overcomer. Be the person who knows the worth of words and how you can encourage people with them. In knowing this, you can start speaking words of truth into your life to help you create the reality you want in it.

Expect your words will encourage the important people in your life. Your hopes for the relationship are hinged on the strength of the connection, so, in all your conversations, encourage them to believe they can expect much from the Lord and that they are conquerors.

You are strong in the name of the Lord. "The name of the Lord is a strong tower; the righteous man runs into it and is safe" (Proverbs 18:10). Nothing can beat that. Nothing else is more reliable. You have to know, beloved, that your Lord and Savior understand what He wants you to speak and do. Many people out there destroy their lives and attract negative consequences to their relationships because of what they speak and do. If they can treat people they are close to rightly, they would be better off.

Your conversation with people can make or break your relationship with them. If you can change your conversation so it can be pleasing to them, your relationship with them will be stronger and better. It starts with what you say. I once had a conversation with a friend of mine, and I said, "When was the last time you heard him speak an encouraging word or say something positive to you. She was like, "I don't receive that from him." The look on her face indicated she was telling the truth, and it made her emotional. Who wouldn't? Imagine recalling the beautiful moment you shared and recalling all the beautiful names he called you when you were still dating; then he finally led you to the altar and all that got thrown to the wind! It takes the bravest of minds to remain emotionless when sweet memories like this come rushing back to your head. It is pretty easy to know those who receive encouragement from their loved ones and those who don't by the look on their faces when sensitive questions like these are asked.

You don't have to say a word when you are encouraged. The look on your face will say it all. When you truly love him or her, give them the encouragement they need. It is frequently said that the highest psychological need of every man is the need to be appreciated. A simple "thank you" or "you look pretty and gorgeous today" can go a long way in making someone's day. That is the thing the people around you want to hear. That is what everyone wants. You should always say words of appreciation to the people who are close to you and share beautiful moments with you. These are the people you should encourage more than anyone else. If you don't know how to invest in making your relationship better by using your conversation, how can you expect to get the maximum benefit out of that relationship? When you do not invest in making yourself a better person, expecting the best is a gross impossibility. It is simply not going to work.

Picture this: do you expect to harvest a beautiful flower when you have not made a conscious effort to cultivate it in the first place? What is it that you believe you've done to deserve this maximum result? As the spiritual man you are, be willing to do these things and let your hopes and expectations be hinged on the faithfulness of the Lord. So have no problem telling your loved ones they are the loveliest thing in the universe. Tell them they're the best thing to happen to you. Place a call to their phones as frequently and as reasonably as you can. Do not say any of these casually because the passion with which you say them matters. Also, encourage them and be as nice to them as possible because whatever happens to them can have a ripple effect on your life. You don't want that!

Get them to travel with you on special occasions. When you are kind to your immediate family—your closest relations—your kindness will be beneficial to their future. Adjustments need to be made if you're not that way with them now, and a large chunk of the responsibility for how they move forward rests on you. We need to make sure our family is as effective as it has to be by making the right adjustments. Luckily, the good Lord has made provisions for all you'll need to make the right decisions for your life. The good Lord has given you the right knowledge to make informed decisions relating to your life and how you interact with those you love and who love you.

It is also important to frequently examine your performance when relating with people. Be honest enough to ask them how they would grade your communication efforts with them. "Do I have an A or a B or a C? What grade are you getting in your relationships? Create a safe environment for them to tell you your "pass score" honestly. This may be the singular most important that you've done in a long while. You'll receive your grade based on how you've been dealing with them all this time. If you want that extraordinary bliss of the kingdom to rub on your relationships, then you must do things differently. You must change the words you use when communicating with the people around you.

So, family, do not forget these points or take them for granted. Apply them in your life and you will notice remarkable changes in brief period of time. To reiterate:

1. The first point dealt with what you perceive about your relationships. This is just about how you see your relationships with people—your employer, the attendant in a grocery store, or the mechanic is fixing your car. What you think and believe about those relationships is what each one is going to be.
2. The second point discussed what an ordinary relationship versus an extraordinary one entails. What type of relationship are you expecting? If you expect your relationship to be extraordinary, you should stop doing ordinary things because ordinary things will only fetch you ordinary results. To do extraordinary things, you need to rely on the words and the will of God.
3. The third point detailed the importance of your speech with the people you interact with on a daily basis, and how it can grossly affect the health of your relationship with them. What have you been saying to the people who are close to you? How were you saying it? The vitality of your speech cannot be overemphasized. What type of grade do you receive in your relationships? If you need things to improve in

your relationships, you need to get busy doing the right things.

None of this advice will work unless there is a commitment on your part to make it work. The relationship will see even more effective results when the commitment is a joint effort between you and whoever you want to grow a stronger tie with. The old saying that two are better than one cannot be any truer.

While it's wisdom to apply all the instructions I've discussed hitherto to make your life better, it is even greater wisdom to thrash things out in the place of prayer. Pray and cast your hope in the Lord. The family that prays together stays together. Prayer is the adhesive that will bond your family together. To this end, pray with your family to increase your faith and get an answer from the Lord.

*"Rejoice in hope, be patient in tribulation, be constant in prayer."*
*—Romans 12:2*

Getting angry over things that can be solved by simple obedience is not wisdom. Selling yourself short to the wrong lifestyle when you can have a better one is not wisdom. Saying awful things to the people around you to "cool off" because you are angry is not wisdom. Doing ordinary things and expecting extraordinary results to flood your life is not wisdom. Do you want a strong life that remains strong even amid the most turbulent storms? Then cast your hopes on the Lord and believe everything He said about you and His promises for your life! Pray and hope on the Lord.

When you are not ashamed of representing God in your life and how you go about your daily affairs, He will surely make you His priority. He'll provide you with an answer to your every question and worries in life. What is that problem you have been struggling with? What is it that you think is too big for God to handle? What is it you're looking for? What is it you're seeking? As the Scriptures have said, whatever you proclaim with your mouth will become your reality. The confessions of your mouth and your heart's beliefs play a great role in what eventually happens in your life. You want to make sure you believe the right things and have the Lord of glory perfect His plans for your life and help you go in the direction He wants you to go.

.

# — 13 —

# BE SELFISH ABOUT BIRTHING GOD'S PROMISES

*The angel said to her, "Do not be afraid, Mary, for you have found favor with God. And behold, you will conceive in your womb and bear a son, and you shall call his name Jesus."*
*—Luke 1:30–31*

Rewards are the hallmark of everything we do on earth. We are all doing something because we hope for something better in return. We all expect that one day, our every engagement will yield the fruits of our expectations. Everyone loves to dream of having have that perfect life someday in the future. When everything we do is about God and not about pleasing ourselves or everyone else, we can expect to have the right results. God is ever gracious and good, and He is willing to be there for us when we give Him a chance. That's who He is, and we can be excited about having a relationship with him. Be excited about encouraging people to be in a relationship with him.

It's all about Him, and when we make Him a priority in our lives, the benefits we stand to gain are astronomical. Do not take for granted those people you have in your space who made Him the center of their lives and relationship. They'll always enjoy the supernatural experience that comes from doing His biddings. Faithful is He who called us unto glory. He is ever there for us when we need Him to be our bearing—to guide us to the destinations we seek. Take insight from the following Bible verse:

> In the sixth month the angel Gabriel was sent from God to a city of Galilee named Nazareth, to a virgin betrothed to a man whose name was Joseph, of the house of David. And the virgin's name was Mary. And he came to her and said, "Greetings, O favored one, the Lord is with you!" But she was greatly troubled at the saying, and tried to discern what sort of greeting this might be. And the angel said to her, "Do not be afraid, Mary, for you have found favor with God. And behold, you will conceive in your womb and bear a son, and you shall call his name Jesus."
>
> —Luke 1:26-31

Mary, the mother of our Lord and Savior, Jesus Christ, was favored among her contemporaries because she prioritized the Lord. Mary was a virgin who knew no man, as it was the norm then to remain chaste and holy. While most of her mates lived to please men, she committed her life wholeheartedly to God, and the reward was massive. The Lord blessed her. He sanctified her womb and made it the placeholder for the forming baby Jesus. What an honor! What other honor can be as great as being the passageway for the Lord of glory, humanity's Savior? Mary's experience can be the same for anyone who makes the Lord a priority in his or her life. The favor of the Lord abounds for any couple who makes God the center of their lives.

Giving birth to the expectations we desire can only be possible when we make the right decisions our priority. What constitutes the right decisions? Do popular suggestions and what we think constitute the right choices? Nothing can be further from the truth. The right choices can only come from doing things in line with God's will. Our opinions, irrespective of how logical they sound, are as inconsequential as a grain of sand on a seashore when compared to the thoughts of the Lord on the subject matter.

Look at your life from the point of view of the process God went through to ensure you get the benefits He wants you to have. Making God our priority is important. You need to have a selfish spiritual mindset to have a great relationship with your partner. This is because what is inside you and what God has given to you is important, and it is what you need to birth a great relationship and have a great life that serves the world by extension.

Having the right mindset will help you give birth to the right results. We need to have the mindset Mary had. We need to make sure we are open and available like Mary was when the angel came to her. She was not startled because she even though she had never been touched and never had intercourse with any man, she trusted God. She had no guilty conscience or feelings. She did not say, "Hey, wait, please, where are you coming from? I need to know more."

She did not utter any of these things because she recognized the messenger of God that was speaking to her, and she said "Okay, I am open to receive it." She had the right mindset to walk this thing out. So in giving birth to your destiny, be like Mary to get the results you are seeking. Anything short of this will not give you the desired results you are expecting.

Be open and available to the spiritual things of the kingdom God wants to give you. You are an innocent person on standby, waiting on God to fill you up to benefit your life. You are inexperienced in this thing. You've never experienced something like this before, and that's why it is always a surprise to us when we finally see the results of what the Lord has placed in our spirit.

When God alone has access to us, He alone places His good gifts in us. Only when we live and walk in Him can He illuminate our mind and change the way we think to align it with the kingdom. Only then can we expect things to work out the way we hope they will. God wants you to have the mindset of the Virgin Mary. He wants you to understand that in order for you to be fulfilled in your life and relationships, you have to acknowledge you cannot do it alone. You don't have enough strength to do things on your own. You need a higher strength—something a mere human being cannot give you.

When you want to give birth to greatness and see things work out the way God means them to, as the Virgin Mary did, there are three things you need to know and come to terms with.

## God's Solutions Are Often Unexpected

The first thing you want to understand is that God's solutions are sometimes unexpected. The thing with God is that He does His thing His way when we least expect it. This is because He is very different from us. He lives in a realm where time and seasons have no influence. We may decide we can figure out when He'll do a thing based on our earthly standards of time and season, but there is no guarantee it will ever line up with when God actually does it.

The realm of possibilities on timing is infinite for God. Biblical history has a lot to say about this. Take Sarah, the wife of Abraham, for example; she got pregnant with Isaac when she least expected it. The same thing rings true for Elizabeth, the mother of John the Baptist, who was called barren. God is not a respecter of man's plans. He does His things in His time and season. That is why you should have a mindset that expects the unexpected when it comes to God, just like the Virgin Mary. When dealing with the things that pertain to your life, place all your hopes on the Lord. Be free with yourself and don't impose any foreign thought or try to force anything.

Because God's timing is unexpected, it is definitely unforeseen—you did not see it coming; and when you don't see it coming, it comes all of a sudden as a wonderful and electrifying happening. It should open your eyes to see something you have never seen before. The angel told Mary she was highly favored of the Lord. It's no wonder when Mary said, "Behold, I am the servant of the

Lord; let it be to me according to your word" (Luke 1:38). That was her mindset, her attitude all the time. You are a blessing unto the world when you receive the things God wants to give you.

## Nurture It

Nurture it. Make sure you value what you have. Consider, for example, women who are in the labor room giving birth to a child. When they are through with the whole process and hold their babies in their arms, they start the long process of nurturing their child well, in line with the ways of the Lord. In the same way, you need to nurture what the Lord gives you.

You'll wash your child every day, and you'll give the baby plenty of healthy food to make sure they build strong bones and a strong immune system. You'll help your baby grow up to become a handsome man or a beautiful woman someday. It is the same with your destiny and purpose. You have to nurture it in order for it to stay alive and grow. Give it a healthy diet. Never overfeed it, which can lead to adverse effects such as obesity. If you underfeed it, it will be malnourished, underdeveloped, and lacking in strength and the will to live. You want to do your part to make sure it grows and develops properly. Your expectations of what is possible will grow to the level to which you feed them.

Whether you're single or married, when God speaks and deals with you, He wants you to nurture your life. Take care of yourself. Encourage yourself. Be focused on making sure you're running after the things He has given to you.

"Fathers, do not exasperate your children; instead, bring them up in the training and instruction of the Lord" (Ephesians 6:4 NIV). God will discipline you, and He wants you to be self-disciplined too. Make sure you're consistent in nurturing the things required of you. He has given you everything you need to nurture the thoughts and aspirations you have for your life, as He has for everyone. At conception, the Lord deposited our potential in us, so we all have the intricate ability to do the things that please him. Invest your all in making sure that it comes out right and that it's pleasing to the Father. As Jesus said, "The one who sent me is with me; he has not left me alone, for I always do what pleases him" (John 8:29). There is a blessing in making sure He receives all the glory. That's why we do what we supposed to do. That's why you should bless your mind by making God's will its center. Start building expectations in the child within you based on God's promises.

## Giving Birth

Giving birth to a wanted child is the happiness of every parent. For such a couple, they follow a set plan and expect a healthy baby. They follow a birthing plan. They make good choices based on the wisdom they can access. Together, they actualize their expectations. Just like the couple expecting to give birth to their first child, you should also expect to give birth to your expectations. This is the type of mindset you need to have.

A baby represents a new beginning. Even in the womb, he or she has life that needs to mature and be delivered. The world is waiting and depending on you to give birth to the thing God has given you. " When a woman is giving birth, she has sorrow because her hour has come, but when she has delivered the baby, she no longer remembers the anguish, for joy that a human being has been born into the world" (John 16:21). A woman in childbirth pushes through the pain toward the goal of giving birth to her child of promise, a child who will be beneficial to the world. God has the same expectation of you.

It is up to you to invest in your life to make it a better one—your life, not the life of another person. The responsibility of taking care of it is on you. Nurture the purpose for which God called you into the world and delivered to you to do.

1. Even though you expect to see your promises fulfilled, God will do it His way in His time—unexpectedly. You can trust His timing. You don't have to force it. It drops upon your life according to the dictates of God.
2. Nurture that which the Lord has given you. Most times, this is squarely your responsibility, but there are times when you will need to help of the Lord to pull through.
3. The third point is the crown of it all; giving birth. Nothing really happened if you don't eventually give birth to your expectations.

Rejoice and then again, rejoice what you have birthed into the world. That's the process of giving birth to your expectations. When you give birth to your expectations, the wise men from the East will come to visit you and present you with gifts, just like they did to Mary when she gave birth to Jesus. It is a reward that the Lord himself will see to. Enjoy it because He wants everything good for you. If your life is important to you, do things right and align your mindset to God's true north to give birth to your purpose.

Heaven's representatives are in this world to help you align with God's purposes for your life. Through the correct understanding of the Scriptures, the men and women of God will equip you to put your hands to the plow to begin every good work. Greater is He who is within you and on you to help you achieve your destined greatness. Commit yourself to the process in faith—the lifeforce that will position your life in the right direction. Faith will help you actualize God's will faster than what would have been possible without it.

# — 14 —

# BE SELFISH ABOUT BEING GRATEFUL

*Greater love has no one than this: that someone lay down his life for his friends.*
*– John 15:13*

Right now, stop whatever you are doing and take a little time to fill your heart and mind with appreciation and gratitude to God for those you have in your life. Give yourself the benefit of being filled with the beauty of life. Mentally project the blessings you've accrued over time, and those within your grasp, because of the people you've met over the years. This moment is the best one to live in, and yes! You are living. Here you are. Think about this!

We have an astronomical number of opportunities within our reach, all thanks to the recent advances in science and technology. We have the ability and freedom to access every type of knowledge, meet a whole lot of people, improve in certain areas of our lives, and learn new things. We are just a click away from a myriad of podcasts and books and Wikipedia pages. Many of us don't have to work with annoying people because we can work from home and interact with our clients online. There are truly a lot of things to appreciate and be grateful for. Oh, how blessed we are.

All the basic things many people take for granted are ours, like having a place to call home and food on the table every day. If for any reason, you were once deprived of either of these, you appreciate and understand the importance of them today, believe me.

Currently, there are millions of people on this planet that would give anything to live the life you are living now. Consider this. They would love to have hot water, indoor plumbing, clean drinking water, electricity, a freezer and a refrigerator, and a bed with clean sheets, blankets, and pillows. You have all this and more. Kindness, nature, music (and the very fact you can even listen to it!), sunshine, the ability to walk and read and write are also things you can appreciate. Enjoy the best life has to offer. Appreciate what you have, no matter how inconsequential you may think it is.

Send a note of appreciation and gratitude to the people who matter to you—to the owner of the place you're living, to the gardener who trims your garden and the plumber who helps fix your pipe when it is faulty. Show them they matter to you through your honest appreciation, either through words or facial expressions. The truth is, we can appreciate absolutely everything when we chose to. It's the little things that make up the bigger picture. Do not wait until someone saves your life for you to show gratitude to them. Thank them now for their everyday acts of kindness.

You can completely turn your day (and life) around when you fill yourself with gratitude. Be grateful for your origins, not just your aspirations, and have a sense of appreciation for the natural turn of things you have experienced in life and how life has always supported you. When you do this very well, your life will align naturally to the goal of sequential order, perfect timing, and manifestation (even if things are difficult until that moment). You'll be quickly filled with deep love, appreciation, and awe about life's operations. It's impossible not to be happy when you see the connecting and organizing energy that the spirit of God demonstrates. He helps you with whatever you focus on. What you set your heart toward is what will manifest as your reality. It is an ancient law of God. The Old Testament writers called it "sowing and reaping." New Age activists love to call it "the law of attraction," a variation of the law of God. If you want happiness to be your lot, set your affections toward being very grateful, honestly grateful for the life you are living, for what you currently have, for the people in your life, and even for the obstacles you've encountered along your journey.

Our words and thoughts are very powerful. They are the creators of our moods and state of mind which are contagious—they can infect the people we interact with in a good or bad way. By concentrating on the greatness of this life, you'll empower yourself and those around you to lead a happier life, and God will respond when you call on His name in prayer. When you pause and consider the life you are living, you'll see how abundant, great, and beautiful life is and all the good it has to offer. The love to lead a pleasing life unto God can also be called gratitude. It is an eternal act that flames up and births the most blessed and interesting life.

Right now, write down about five things you are eternally grateful for. They can be the situations you find yourself in, the people you are surrounded with, just anything that counts. Truly feel your gratitude and appreciation for them, and see how honestly blessed you are for possessing those things and knowing those people. So much. The simple act of constantly redirecting your mind to concentrate on the positive part of things instead of the negative part improves your mood. And when you change the way you see a situation, the way the situation appeared will also change. Appreciate the people you constantly associate with. It is in your best interest to feel and think in terms of gratitude all day. When you do, you'll see radical transformations and very strong shifts in all parts of your life.

## — 15 —

# BE SELFISH ABOUT CHASING YOUR DREAMS

*On the third day a wedding took place at Cana in Galilee. Jesus's mother was there, and Jesus and his disciples had also been invited to the wedding.*

*– John 2:11*

Moses ran after the things God gave him because He provided him with clear instructions to do those things, and there was no question Moses was going to do them. You want to have a relationship with God like Moses had. You want to be a dream chaser, chasing after the Father's will in your life. You can tell the difference between dream chasers and the rest of the world because of how specific their chase of God can be and how alive and full of God's energy they are. The richest place in the world is the graveyard because it's a collection of human potential that will never materialize anything. A dead man will remain a dead man and nothing can be done about it. But we are alive in Christ! "Consider yourselves dead to sin and alive to God in Christ Jesus" (Romans 6:11).

People keep chasing their tail, wondering if there's clarity in the things they are doing because all they hear are the riddles and not the face-to-face, clear instruction Moses got. God deals with you face-to-face if you are as close to Him as Moses was. There's no question about the instructions God gives you.

There are three ways God can speak to you face-to-face and give you a clear instruction for your life the way He did for Moses. They are:

## He Gives You an Idea

When God gives you an idea, it is like no other. It comes from a place no human mind can ever comprehend. When God places a purpose in your heart, it blows your mind. What the world offers is only a fraction of what the God of angel armies will put in your mind as an idea.

The first thing you will be surprised at is how seemingly mighty the task appears. It is often said that if you know what God has called you to do, you will immediately reject it on the grounds that it is beyond your ability. You may ask Him, "Is this something you have called me to do? I can't believe you would think I can accomplish such a thing!" Drop your inferiority complex and put all your trust in Him. Irrespective of what you think or what your opinion is, God believes it is possible or He wouldn't have asked you to do it. That is the reality of the realm where He resides; there is no impossibility in Him. He gives you an idea that He believes is possible.

He believes you have a target to meet and He will empower you to meet that target. You are a dream chaser. Go hunt your dreams!

He wants you to run after this thing. "Don't you know that you are God's temple and that God's Spirit dwells in your midst? If anyone destroys God's temple, God will destroy that person; for God's temple is sacred, and you together are that temple" (I Corinthians 3:16–17).

Understand how God sees you. You are a godly temple He constructed. He has put you together with great care and workmanship to accomplish what He planned for you even before you were born. No man can place this purpose in your mind. When you understand your purpose is from Him, your mindset can be likened to that of Moses. God will give you the mindset when you stand face-to-face with Him and hear Him speak!

God will confer the great dexterity and agility you need to carry out your purpose, so no man can take it from you or give you a superior one. Place your heart fully into it, and don't try quitting. It will all come to pass because it came from God.

The book of Numbers says the Lord called Aaron, Miriam, and Moses out to tell them there was a difference in the way He communicated with Moses versus the way He communicated with other people. While the Lord communicated with the other people in dreams and riddles, He communicated with Moses with clarity and, most importantly, face-to-face (Numbers 12:1–3). Moses's obedience and humble disposition was the reason why he heard the clear instructions from God. The spirit of God was inside him. He was faithful to the idea God gave him, and then after understanding that idea, God built upon it by giving him the ability to think more clearly than his contemporaries could.

## Imagination

Moses thought outside of the box, building on the idea God gave him. God gave him the ability to produce and assimilate a spiritual idea. When you can assimilate a spiritual idea, you can materialize the imagination that comes to your heart from the Lord. Imagination and ideas go hand-in-hand.

The mind is the medium through which we all function. It jumps from place to place like a restless kid or a monkey. That is the mind's basic tendency. Yet true grandeur lies in placing your mind under the control of God's spirit in you. Having God's spirit is like having the world's most powerful computer at your disposal. A computer that matches the human mind's capabilities has never been developed, but if it's ever built, conservative estimates say it could only fit into a building with thirty-three stories! Only the spirit of God can create something that significant. There are two reasons why you need to build your ability to imagine:

1. The first and long-term one is to calm the mind. A peaceful mind generates energy, and only the Lord can provide you with one.
2. Imagination captures your mind's fancy for a more short-term result and uses the energy generated to steer your mind to the right course.

Relying on the Word of God to help you master your mind is the key to mastering yourself. Many successful Christians have attributed their relational success to their imaginative ability.

When you grab hold of this imagination thing, it excites you and places you and your relationships on the path God has designated. Living out your purpose has to do with your connection to the initial idea God gave you. Only then can you build your imagination. "Whatever you ask in prayer, believe that you have received it, and it will be yours." (Mark 11:24). "All things for which you pray and ask, believe that you have received them, and they will be granted you" (NASB).

God is going to give you an image of your future that's going to blow your mind. It doesn't matter what man might say to you, just hold on to what God has spoken over your life, and when you hold on to those things, you will look back over your life to the things you have through you and see how much He has helped you.

He has plans for your life only if you let Him be at the center of it. You don't have to give a second thought about what the world thinks about you. All that matters is that you are doing the things that are pleasing to God. God has an idea for you that is encapsulated in imagination. That's a process that's completely different to one the world may suggest. But it doesn't matter. All that matters is that you are using this faculty the Lord provided you with to the best of your ability.

## He Will Give You an Idea

All great inventions and achievements began in the form of an idea. Imagination is what births ideas. While imagination itself is very important, you have to be a true spiritual dream chaser to get God's ideas. You need to have a detailed plan to ensure you accomplish the purposes the Lord has called you to achieve.

This is a spiritual ability God has given unto you. "The heart of man plans his way, but the Lord established his steps" (Proverbs 16:9). When you put your plans together with God, your footsteps will be ordered by Him. Every step you take will be on His list as long as you don't give up on Him.

To be a dream chaser, you need to listen to your spirit and encourage yourself. There are periods when you may feel down or discouraged with life. It is your business to make sure you are well catered for emotionally. You cannot give up on yourself. You have to stand strong when you are weak. If you feel a matter is beyond what you can handle, take it up to God in prayer and He will answer you. He is ever faithful, and He is true. He will be there for you when you call upon His name. Be like Moses, who was the delight of the Lord. Seek clarity from the good Lord and let Him be responsible for the direction of your relationships. Don't force things to happen and let the will of God gradually unfold as He has purposed. This is *His* plan for your life. Stick to it and see how wonderful your life will turn out to be.

When you are a dream chaser, you will be accountable for what God has put inside you. You will be successful because success is the lot of whoever believes in God. You cannot give up, and you cannot quit.

The things the Lord gives you an instruction to do is what He will give you the grace to pull through. All you have to do is to cast your cares on Him for He cares for you.

Let God expand your imagination, but most importantly, stick to the plan He gave you. When you do these three things, your dream of having a great destiny will be speedily accomplished. God bless you all!

# IN CLOSING

We can alter our relationships to create a new future when we understand how and why it is important to align ourselves with God's will. There is a law raging in every one of us that is seeking to be expressed. This law is why there is blessedness on the faces of many happy people you see on the street. It is the reason why a lot of seeming wonders exist in our world today. It is also why you will get to your destination and be anywhere you want to be. Because you can align with Him and harness yourself to this advantage, ask the Lord for almost anything and He will grant it to you. We are all a product of who we have considered ourselves to be and how much of God we factor into our lives.

Dennis S. Nickens

# ABOUT THE AUTHOR

Dennis S. Nickens, MBA, is the CEO of Total Package LLC, a relatiobship-building company. He is also a program analyst with the federal government, a service member, and the author of two books: *Doing It God's Way, It Works: Friendship transitioning into a healthy marriage* and *Unbroken Vows: Keeping it together.*

Dennis's parents played an active role in his development growing up, modeling commitment to God above all. He saw how it affected not only their marriage for the better, but also the lives of everyone they came in contact with. From this experience, he learned that anything that's worth having is going to require persistence and commitment.

Also known as "the spiritual Romeo," it is Dennis's purpose in life to run the race he has been called to run—to encourage couples and assist them in believing that they have a right to the Tree of Life, along with the authority to demand and expect that God's promises will come to pass and work out in their favor. A devoted husband and a believer in the Most High, Dennis believes that every relationship has the opportunity to be something amazing, but that both participants are required to put forth the effort to make it happen.

Dennis's motto in life is: "It's not about me, it's all about Him." Jesus is the one who died for him, so He is the one his life should be about. He knows that the more he understands who He is, the better off his relationships will be. The same goes for you.

## Follow Dennis

Website: www.tpllc2020.us
Email: tpllc2020@gmail.com

# ACKNOWLEDGEMENTS

son.

# Can You Help?

Reviews are everything to an author because they mean a book is given more visibility. If you enjoyed this book, please review it on your favorite book review sites and tell your friends about it. Thank you!

www.ingramcontent.com/pod-product-compliance
Lightning Source LLC
LaVergne TN
LVHW010107170826
845678LV00012B/2275

* 9 7 9 8 8 9 5 6 9 0 3 7 6 *